TRINIDAD & TOBAGO

A Caribbean Expression of Colourful Diversity

EDISON BOODOOSINGH

Plain Vision Publishing

1962 - 2012

TRINIDAD & TOBAGO

International Standard Book Number 978-0-9761628-7-2

Library of Congress Control Number: 2011929801

EDISON BOODOOSINGH

Photographs © 2012, Edison Boodoosingh
Text © 2012, Emmanuel Guadeloupe

Published by
PLAIN VISION PUBLISHING
New York, NY, USA
& Chaguanas, Trinidad & Tobago
Website: www.pvppress.com
Email: info@plainvisionpublishing-pvp.com

Graphics Design by:
Anthony Carr of Bezalel Designs

Printed in the United States of America.
All rights reserved under International Copyright law.
Contents and/or cover may not be reproduced in whole
or in part without prior written permission.

Contents

Foreword vii
Preface ix
Map of Trinidad and Tobago x

Introduction 2

People & Culture 6
    The People of Trinidad &Tobaga 10
    People & Culture Sports 27
    People & Culture - Foods 28
    The French Creole and Spanish Flavours of Trinidad 30
    Tobago – The Mystique of Its Beauty 38
    African Cultural Dance 54
    East Indian Cultural Dance 62
    Multi-Cultural & Contemporary Dance 67
    The Drums of Trinidad and Tobago 74
    Calypso, Soca & Chutney Music of Trinidad & Tobago 81

Architecture & Monuments 84
    Colonial Government House of Colour 93
    Monumental Expressions of Faith 98
    Temple in the Sea 104

National Festivals & Observances 110
    Kalinda – Stick Fighting 111
    Canboulay 114
    Carnival Trinbagonian Style 117
    Traditional & Modern Masquerade Characters 121
    Phagwa 150
    Spiritual Shouter Baptists Liberation Day 154
    Christian Celebrations of Easter 157

    La Divina Pastora & Soparee Mai 160
    Mud Volcano Puja 162
    Ganga Dhara 163
    Corpus Christi Processions 166
    St. Peter's Day 168
    Emancipation 170
    Eid-ul-Fitr 172
    Amerindian Heritage Day 174
    Orisha Worship 176
    Ramleela 179
    Divali – Festival of Lights 184
    Kartik Snaan 186
    Hosay 188
    Chinese Festivals 191
    Christmas in Trinidad and Tobaga 194

Eco-Systems & Natural Wonders 196
    Land of the Double Chaconia 208
    The Giant Leatherback Turtle 218

Commerce & Industry 222
    Drilling for Oil Since 1857 228

Sights & Scenes 248
    Caribbean Coconuts 255

The Ever Evolving Faces of the Races 260
    The Faces of the Races 260

Bibliography 268
Sources & References 268

Preamble Pages Pictures

The Repsol Building, **Queen's Park,** Port of Spain iv

Sunset at Pigeon Point, Tobago vi

Colourful Carnival masquerader viii

Cover picture (front and back spread)
Maracas Bay

Foreword

Photography is the emphasis of Boodoosingh's book, **_TRINIDAD & TOBAGO – A Caribbean Expression of Colourful Diversity._** The photographer seeks to give a probing pictorial perspective into the natural, social, economic and cultural character of this fascinating Caribbean nation of some 1.3 million people. The book is organised into seven sections: People & Culture, Architecture & Monuments, National Festivals & Observances, Eco-systems & Natural Wonders, Commerce & Industry, Sights & Scenes and The Ever Evolving Faces of the Races. Whilst the vast array of wonderful photographs is the chief protagonist in the narrative of this book, there is a complementing balance of a well written series of insightful and informative supplemental articles and captions which give a qualified literary dimension.

This pictorial reportage gives a 'through-the-lens' view of the modern face of the culture of Trinidad and Tobago. It is a perspective that captures facets of daily life which are based on a remarkable mixture of historical and social elements. These components are principally derived from a rich vein of sub-cultures such as the aboriginal Amerindians, Western Europeans, West Africans, East Indians, Chinese, Middle Easterners and sundry extra regional influences. This unique blend of cultural ingredients is a result of the great demographic redistribution and population infusion of the region which began during the nation's formative years in the modern era, roughly between the 16th and the 19th centuries.

Geographically and ecologically, from the seaside, the country plains and into the lush hillside regions, the photographer snaps a broad and enthralling range of the nation's natural habitat. This kaleidoscope of features makes up a series of varied and expansive biological systems and scenic landscapes which form the rich environmental complex of Trinidad and Tobago.

The stunning photography across the pages of this volume gives a compelling and discerning visual commentary of this unique Caribbean nation. The wide assortment of colourful images highlights the intricate cultural network of people and places, along with, characters and customs, mingling in a common social habitat. The surrounding backdrop is adorned with elaborate facades of tropical flora and fauna. It is altogether, a beautiful presentation of Trinidad and Tobago.

Preface

Recently I attended a lecture on the history of the Muslim event of Hosay held in St. James, Port of Spain, presented by Dr. Satnarine Balkaransingh in association with the National Library and Information Services (NALIS). During the presentation, he asked the audience, which included a number of secondary school children, how many had ever attended a Hosay celebration event. To my surprise only a couple of hands were raised. Given my own interest in the many wonderful cultural activities which our nation has to offer, I anticipated a greater response from those gathered.

The impact of the rich culture of Trinidad and Tobago remains largely under appreciated, even by many of its own people! It can be argued that this southern-most Caribbean island nation bears an extra regional character distinct from most other islands. The signature of the national identity comes from the unique proportional mix of ethnicities flavoured by their inherent sub-cultures. There is so much more on offer here to engage the attention beyond beaches, eco-systems, architectural structures and even the commercial wealth of the oil and gas industry.

To really know Trinidad and Tobago is to experience the captivating fusion of the drums of Hosay; the duelling of the Kalinda Stick Fighters; the colours of Phagwa; the drama of Ramleela; the curious spectacle of goat racing; the '*picong*' in the songs of calypso, soca and chutney; 'doubles' from Curepe Junction or Debe; the passion of religious observances; or, the lights of Divali and Christmas. There is the pageantry and merriment of Carnival that is like no other and the many more rich cultural performances across the length and breadth of this intriguing country. These all give uninhibited insights into the very heart of the nation. Over the years I have developed a personal delight in capturing photographic images of my land. I find that I am now inspired to share my photography with my fellow *Trinbagonians,* and anyone else, to showcase some of the amazing virtues of this twin-island Caribbean state.

It is my hope that in viewing this compilation of featured images, both young and old would be challenged to look beyond their immediate circles of interest. Let there be an enthusiasm to see and learn about the many festivals of the land. May there be less inhibition to witness religious activities outside one's own faith, whether Christian, Hindu or Muslim. I encourage everyone to experience the wonders of our cultural dance, theatre, African drums and East Indian tassa at events like the Best Village competitions. See the elaborate Moriah wedding and Cocoa dancing among other events at the Tobago Heritage Festival. Whilst the Carnival is truly a massive extravaganza, it is not the sole cultural expression of Trinidad and Tobago. With 280 pages of vivid colour photographs, I have tried to paint a broader picture of the cultural landscape of this fascinating nation. At our local institutes of learning, studies in our own culture should feature as prominently as Pythagoras. In such a case, greater levels of value for our heritage and capabilities are more likely to be encouraged and pursued.

The photography in this book has taken me over six years to compile. It is based on expression, colour, composition and lots of walking! Having now completed this first book, out of the vast collection of more photographs, I will be attempting to delve much deeper into the festivals, observances, cultural expressions, sights and scenes of this land in books to follow.

I hope you enjoy this work on, **TRINIDAD & TOBAGO –** *A Caribbean Expression of Colourful Diversity.*

In Memory

This book is dedicated to the loving memory of my grandmother Mildred Dhanesar, my mother, Rosina Mohammed, my step father, Hollis Lalsingh and, Debra Franco, my sister whose battle with cancer ended in 2012. "Absence in the body is presence with the Lord." May we meet again.

Edison Boodoosingh

TRINIDAD & TOBAGO

Introduction

As if by very deliberate design, the exact geographical location of Trinidad and Tobago appears central in contributing to the extraordinary diversity of its cultural, commercial and even ecological evolution. Seemingly suspended at the southern end of the Caribbean chain of islands and perched a mere seven miles off the north east coast of the South American mainland, Trinidad and Tobago stands as a key hemisphere gateway. It is the habitat of a population of approximately 1.3 million people, along with some of the most spectacular flora and fauna found anywhere on earth. Also, it is consolidating upon its reputation as a strategic international trading junction serving as an interchange of wide-ranging socio-economic and environmental enterprises. Together, these components provide a distinct blend that embodies the colourful life of this vibrant and progressive nation.

At the pin-point latitude and longitude coordinates of 10° 40' North and 61° 31' West, you will find yourself downtown in the capital city of Port of Spain, the pulsating national nerve centre which showcases every imaginable thought provoking sight, sound and sensation. The peculiar natural location of this 5,128 km² combined land mass of Trinidad and Tobago, has significantly influenced the historical foundation of its cultural development by hosting some of the great explorers of old. To the indigenous Amerindian Arawak and Carib people from the South American Orinoco delta region, Trinidad was known as *Kairi, the Land of the Humming Bird.* Tobago was called *Tavaco,* the probable origin of the Spanish word 'tabaco', which in turn provided the English word 'tobacco'. Tavaco was the Carib's word for a long-stemmed pipe with two nose pieces used for smoking the leaf that grew in abundance on the island. Later, Christopher Columbus, with his journeys from Spain to the *New World,* arrived and gave Trinidad the name, *Trinidad,* which has remained to this day. He also called Tobago, *La Bella Forma,* a name which lasted only briefly in the island's history. Over the years to contemporary times, Trinidad and Tobago's geographical location has attracted a profusion of multi-ethnic travellers from distant lands including Europe, Africa, India, China and the Middle East to make this vivacious twin island nation their home.

As a consequence of its varied social and natural history, Trinidad and Tobago offers a unique Caribbean confluence of cosmopolitan culture, commerce and ecosystems which are intricately intertwined to form a most engaging geopolitical melange. A comparatively prosperous country, its working nationals enjoy an above average per capita income level. Trinidad and Tobago also attracts a broad cross-section of visitors, not only to its world acclaimed annual Carnival 'jump-up', but to a range of international business and commercial activities in its significant oil and gas industry. Other forward looking mercantile interests include its burgeoning manufacturing, banking, arts, tourism, technology and agriculture sectors.

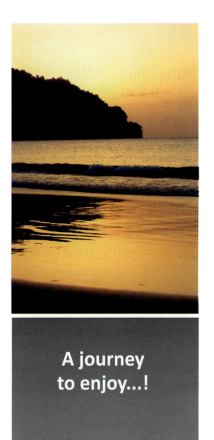

A journey to enjoy...!

Among the featured natural wonders and diverse ecosystems, the Main Ridge Forest Reserve in the central highlands of Tobago is recognized as the oldest protected Rain Forest in the Western Hemisphere. Within this area, nature lovers will be awed by a biodiversity that includes some 210 species of birds, 123 species of butterflies, 24 types of snakes, 17 species of bats, 16 species of lizards and 14 species of frogs. Over in Trinidad, there is the famous Pitch Lake, considered one of the natural wonders of the world. This phenomenon can be found in

Panoramic view of the city of Port of Spain from Fort George

the south western reaches of the island. It is the largest of three asphalt lakes in the world. In 1595 the famous English mariner and explorer, Sir Walter Raleigh, is said to have moored his ship off the coast, near the location now called La Brea, in order to get some of this tar-like substance to seal the hull of his vessel. The lake covers an area of approximately 42 hectares reaching about 80 metres deep at the centre. The Pitch Lake is said to have reserves of up to eight million tonnes of asphalt. Assuming the present rate of excavation, it will take more than 400 years before its reserves are exhausted.

Another prominent natural attraction in Trinidad and Tobago is the nesting of the famous giant Leatherback Turtles from March to August each year. At the height of the season, hundreds of these migratory turtles, considered sacred by some, return from far flung oceans around the world to lay their eggs on local beaches. Grande Riviere and other locations along Trinidad's north and east coasts, as well as beaches in Tobago, are popular nesting havens.

This book, **Trinidad & Tobago – A Caribbean Expression of Colourful Diversity,** offers an insightful photographic tour which gives an exciting visual perspective of some of the marvellous and enchanting scenes of this twin island paradise. As you thumb through these pages, you will see wonderful images featuring the People and Culture; National Festivals & Observances; Architecture and Monuments; Eco-Systems and Natural Wonders; Commerce and Industry; and, Sights and Scenes.

Enjoy the journey...!

People & Culture

With the unwavering and unmatched 'Trinbagonian' passion and expression... Despite the challenges, it's always, "Doh worry 'bout dat..."

The identity of a nation lies in the hearts of its nationals and is visible in their faces.

Familiarly known as *'Trinis'* or *'Trinbagonians'*, the people of Trinidad and Tobago personify a unique culture that has evolved out of a distinct multi-ethnic convergence. They are the by-products of a fate rising out of the events of many bold deeds committed by a range of historical adventurers. The pursuits of these explorers included the exploits of the pre-Columbian Amerindian people launching out beyond the shores of their South American Orinoco jungle homelands to the islands of the Caribbean Sea; European colonists seeking to expand into new geographical territories; navigators charting alternate maritime trading routes; prospectors of the infamous *El Dorado* - the gold of the Americas; slave traders; migrants fleeing social persecutions in their native countries; and, entrepreneurs of lucrative cultivations of cotton, indigo, sugar, tobacco, and cocoa.

The endeavours of these travellers to this *"New World"* unwittingly contributed to the unifying of an unlikely mix of ethnicities including Amerindians, Spanish, French, British, Dutch, Africans, Portuguese, East Indians, Chinese, Syrians and Lebanese – the people who comprise *Trinbagonian* nationals of today. The famed Latin motto of *'E Pluribus Unum'* – out of many one, is as applicable to Trinidad and Tobago as it is anywhere else in the world.

The culture of Trinidad and Tobago is the fruit of its people's communal determination. Over the expanse of time, their ancestors withstood fierce adversity including being dislodged from distant homelands, perilous voyages by sea, all manner of diseases, slavery, subjection to indentured labour, various forms of social exploitation and having to determine life in unfamiliar and whole new environments. Pressed to survive, they resolved to discover and fashion creative ways to sustain their total being. From work to play, they ensured that they would preserve an existence over the period of their very traumatic set of historical circumstances. All aspects of the many-faceted *Trinbagonian* identity today have been painstakingly carved out of the experiences its people have endured over the past centuries. The nation's heritage has been purchased with the precious blood, sweat and tears of all its multi-ethnic forefathers to produce what is known today as Trinidad and Tobago. Present-day *Trinbagonians* therefore carry an important responsibility to cherish, conserve and consolidate upon the nation's hard-earned cultural legacies for future generations. It is a national quest that must prevail, despite the weathering forces of the eroding winds of globalization in this ever changing age of information and communication carried on the wings of modern technology.

Like high octane fuel, the full-bodied ethnic diversity of Trinidad and Tobago is a principal contributor which energizes the national character. It is recognized by the indomitable and irrepressible national joy and vitality which shine like a beacon of hope. Regardless of adverse conditions, *Trinbagonians* have an uncanny ability to navigate a transforming course to happy

People casting the same shade

survival. Perhaps it is the evolution of a built-in self-preserving quality. In whatever way this capacity is defined, there is a continued manifestation of the creative adaptability of *Trinbagonians* to prevail whatever the circumstances.

With the unwavering and unmatched '*Trinbagonian*' passion and expression… Despite the challenges, it's always, **"Doh worry 'bout dat…"**

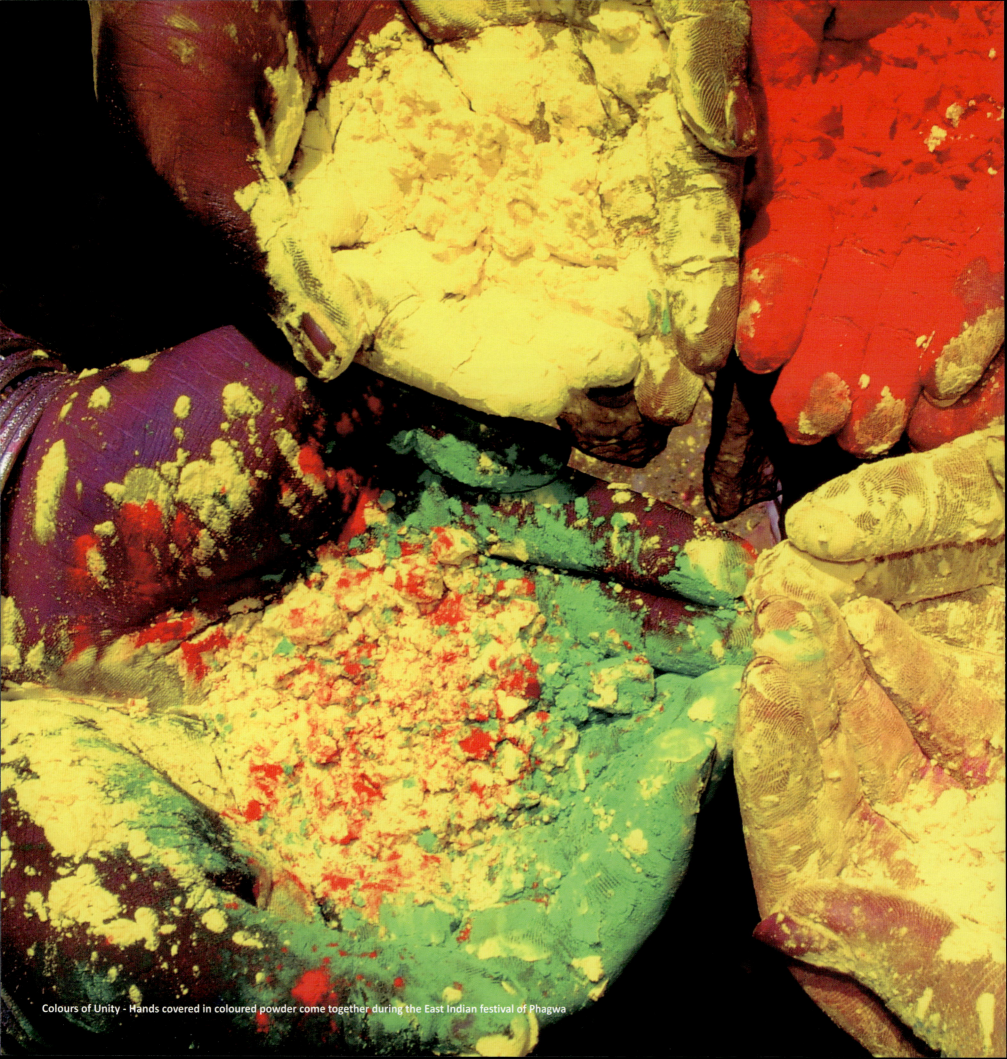

Colours of Unity - Hands covered in coloured powder come together during the East Indian festival of Phagwa

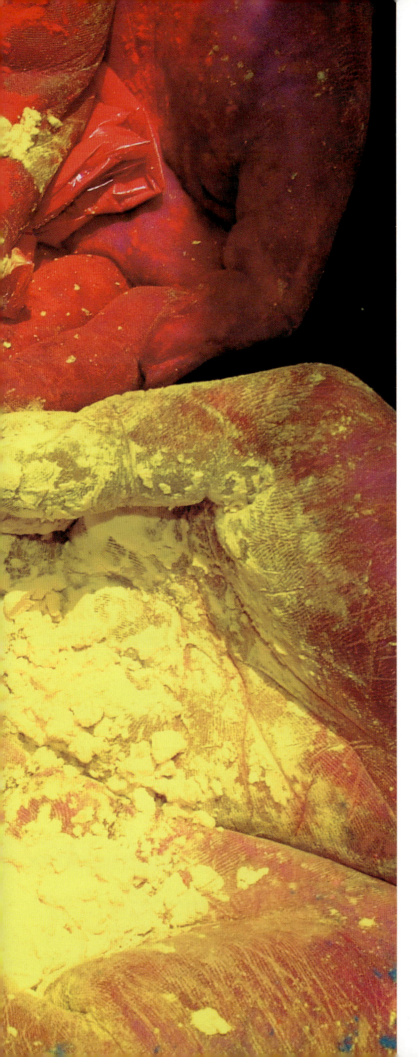

The People of Trinidad and Tobago

Who are Trinbagonians?

The colourful citizenry of Trinidad and Tobago can collectively be ranked very highly among the most multi-ethnic and multi-community populations anywhere in the world. The character and driving force of the people who occupy the 5,128km^2 landmass of this remarkable twin-island state have a distinctly diverse social profile. *Trinbagonians* are represented in a broad demographic amalgamation distributed among the predominant East Indian and African descendant groupings complemented by significant numbers claiming origins from British, Spanish, French, Chinese, Syrian, Lebanese, Portuguese, Italian, Amerindian and an assortment of mixed ancestries.

Throughout history, the many combinations of fate triggered a staggered immigration pattern to the shores of these southernmost Caribbean islands. The in-bound journeys featured adventure, commercial pursuits, exploitation, seeking a haven from social persecution and still many more reasons for heading to Trinidad and Tobago. Waves of migrants landed. The conquests of the Amerindians were early forerunners to the European colonists and their accompanying enslaved labour-force, and others, caught in varying migratory endeavours. Different categories of travellers brought their own set of social complexes which continue to contribute to creating the unique *Trinbagonian* identity. Apart from the primary layers of races in the cross-section of the total national veneer, the compacted character of the cultural structure of Trinidad and Tobago requires a very discerning eye to distinguish and identify the many nuances of its individual social components. The following list of people provides a revealing insight into the wide ethnic make-up of the local masses:

Amerindian Trinidadians and Tobagonians

Though now a comparatively minuscule proportion of the total population of Trinidad and Tobago, the descendants of the Amerindian people from the South American mainland, namely Caribs and Arawaks, are undeniably recognized as the first inhabitants of these islands. Archaeological artefacts inform that the Eastern Caribbean was first populated by these aboriginal Americans from as early as 3500 to 4000 BC. Hidden within the recesses of their DNA, they possess cultures that were developed over many centuries in the Amazon and Orinoco river valley regions of what is now Venezuela, The Guyanas, and Brazil, that have made an indelible mark upon the Islands.

The Carib people have outlasted their Arawak relatives as they proved themselves to be more resilient in the face of the many ravages of change over time. Through the ages, they have survived as successful farmers on produce such as cassava, corn, tobacco, beans, squash and other crops. They also relied on hunting, fishing, and foraging for other dietary items. Additionally, they were active voyagers, skilled at navigating the mainland rivers and the open seas that linked the islands with one another.

When Christopher Columbus and the Spanish colonizers arrived in the Caribbean, the native population throughout the entire Antillean archipelago was estimated to be around four million people. However, a great decline in these figures occurred due to the devastating effects from the combination of warfare, enslavement, exposure to unfamiliar diseases, general abuse and ruthless colonial practices perpetrated upon them.

In Trinidad today there are around 12,000 people with direct traces of Amerindian descent living primarily in the north-eastern region of the country. There remains a notable Carib influence across the nation with a host of towns and villages that have retained their indigenous names including Arima, Caroni, Carapichaima, Chaguanas, Chaguaramas, Couva, Cunupia, Curepe, Guayaguayare, Icacos, Iere Village, Maracas, Mayaro, Mucurapo, Tabaquite, Tacarigua, Toco and many others. The Santa Rosa Carib festival celebrated in Arima is a significant commemoration which highlights the indigenous ancestry of this land. The mystique of the Carib, or *Kalinago* people as they are also known, still permeates the land. As a symbol of a storied era, the statue of the legendary Carib warrior, Hyarima, with battle spear in hand, casts a commanding gaze over the nation from his Arima look-out.

European Trinidadians and Tobagonians

There is an array of Trinidad and Tobago nationals of European descent. Many can trace their heritage to West European countries such as England, France, Germany, Ireland, Italy, Portugal, Scotland and Spain. The first arrivals of the forefathers of these citizens started in the 16th century. Throughout the following years to the present time, other Europeans have journeyed and settled in the islands. Of these *Trinbagonians*, the major group is of British descent, followed by Spanish, French and Portuguese; and to a lesser extent, Italian, German and Scandinavian.

At the onset of the modern era, Spain was the first European country to lay claim to Trinidad and take rule for three centuries. For commercial purposes, they formed alliances with the French in the neighbouring Caribbean territories, Portugal and other European countries, who shared a similar Roman Catholic faith. They offered incentives of land ownership to their fellow colonists to come and develop profitable plantations in the country. Those who accepted the offer, over time, generally did succeed in this venture and grew in economic and social status.

In 1797, as part of the expansion of their empire, the British took over rule of Trinidad from the Spanish. Though the island was now under English speaking administrative governance, more than 80% of the island's population still spoke French, Creole or Spanish. It was not until the early part of the 20th century that the prevalent use of the *Franco-Afro-Ibero* languages began to decline and be replaced by English.

Leading into and beyond the national milestone of independence in 1962, generations of Europeans have remained in Trinidad and live mostly in areas in and around Port of Spain, towns along the Northern Range and certain locations in the centre and south of the island. Recent years have seen the idyllic settings of Tobago attracting many European retirees who have come to make this island nation their home. They have migrated from Germany, England, Scotland, Sweden, Norway, Denmark, Holland and elsewhere in Europe bolstering the balance in the spectrum of colour among the people of Trinidad and Tobago.

African Trinidadians and Tobagonians

The deep full-bodied influence of Africans in Trinidad and Tobago began when, as slaves, they were first brought to the island in 1517 by Spanish Colonists. As the Amerindian population was facing annihilation in the Caribbean, African slaves were imported in great numbers to fill the labour needs on the various plantations in the effort towards commercializing and profiting from the colonies.

The colonists proved that Africans could survive when they were introduced into the Caribbean because this new habitat was quite similar to their indigenous West African tropical environment. The arrival of *Yoruba, Igbo, Asante, Fon, Mande* and *Mandingo* people indicate that slaves were drawn from a wide area across West Africa. West Africans were quite familiar with farming crops that included rice, peanuts, bananas and root vegetables like yams and dasheen. They were also hunters who had a close affinity with the land and could readily adapt to the natural environment. Those formative years demonstrated that Africans were very resilient. However, it was these same tough human qualities which were exploited by their colonist masters on the vast sugar and cocoa plantations for great profit. These durable attributes would equally and eventually carry them beyond servitude to self-determined liberation. The British Parliament passed the Slave Trade Act of 1807 that abolished the trading of slaves, and the Slavery Abolition Act of 1833 legally abolished the practice of slavery.

Today, African *Trinbagonians* make up the country's second largest ethnic group which provides a certain rich cultural depth of colour and complexion to the nation's identity.

East Indian Trinidadians and Tobagonians

Originating from the sub-continent of Asia, East Indian *Trinbagonians* now make up the country's largest single ethnic group. They are primarily descendants of indentured workers from India, brought as a new stable workforce to replace the freed African slaves who refused to continue working on the sugar plantations.

In May 1845, the first East Indians arrived in Trinidad from the British Raj, as India was then known, being a colony within the British Empire. The *Fatel Rozack* would be the first of many ships to transport over 140,000 East Indians to Trinidad between 1845 and 1917. Many of them were drawn from provinces of eastern Uttar Pradesh and western Bihar thus reflecting differences in caste, customs and languages. However, as they steadily transitioned from East to West, their will to survive and thrive helped them to determine a dignity that has withstood the test of time.

A second wave of East Indian migrants came to Trinidad after the abolition of indentured servitude in 1917. The majority of people who came at this time did so by personal choice. Pursuing a better way of life, they sought to ply their skills as doctors, entrepreneurs, and in other professional exploits. Most of these East Indians maintained many more aspects of their indigenous culture as they enjoyed far less stringent conventions than their compatriots who had arrived in earlier years.

The East Indian population of Trinidad and Tobago can be found spread all across the nation. However, there are popular concentrations in towns and villages in Central and South Trinidad. Some of these locations even bear names from their country of origin, for example: Fyzabad, Golconda, Delhi Road, Barrakpore, Hindustan, Madras and Calcutta. All these sultry eastern names create a sense of a typical sub-continent flavour to this Caribbean twin-island nation.

Portuguese Trinidadians and Tobagonians

Trinbagonians of Portuguese descent have a notable place in the historical development of Trinidad and Tobago. Dating back to the days of Columbus, many Portuguese migrated to the Caribbean driven by different motivations. Some immigrated because of economic reasons, whilst others left Portugal due to adverse religious and political circumstances. The main influx of Portuguese people into the Caribbean, and in particular to Trinidad, came in the 19th century. The majority of these immigrants were drawn from the Portuguese Atlantic provinces of the Azores, Madeira and the Cape Verde Islands. Among these, the largest group of people was from the Madeira Islands, a small archipelago situated in the Atlantic Ocean off the north-west African coast of Morocco.

Though belonging to the western European grouping of descendants in Trinidad and Tobago in geo-political terms, these Portuguese Madeirans came to the Caribbean not as colonizers or plantation owners, but essentially as contributors to the labouring workforce. Their major entry to the region coincided with the abolition of slavery and the consequential need for workers to replace the freed African slaves. Predating, first the Chinese migrants, and then the East Indian indentured workers, in working on the cocoa and sugar estates, the Madeiran people proved less suited to plantation work. As a result, they left the agricultural fields for other enterprises. Relying on their innate business skills, they took up work in and around the cities of Port of Spain and San Fernando as shop-keepers, rum shop owners, winemakers, bakers and other trades which more mirrored their way of life back in Madeira.

Today, *Trinbagonians* of Portuguese descent are an integral part of the national landscape. Their visible presence spans the entire spectrum of the political, economic and social life of Trinidad and Tobago.

Chinese Trinidadians and Tobagonians

The quintessential *Chinese Shop, Chinese Laundry* and *Chinese Restaurant* have a very fond place within the lore and societal development of Trinidad and Tobago. Of course the Chinese community here goes far beyond those traditional labels with an important *Chinese-Trinbagonian* presence in the ranks of lawyers, doctors, politicians, accountants, artists and various other kinds of highly-skilled professionals across the social landscape.

The entry of Chinese immigrants to Trinidad and Tobago came mainly during four distinct periods. The first episode of October 1806 saw 192 of 200 surviving their journey to Trinidad, sailing on the British ship, the *Fortitude*. They came from the Chinese regions of Macao, Penang and Canton. With the abolition of slavery about to take effect, the British government and plantation owners sought to find new workers to replace the African slaves who had exercised their new-found right to no longer work as forced labourers on the estates. These Chinese immigrants were being considered to fill the gap as peasant farmers to maintain productivity on the sugar plantations. However, the venture did not succeed as envisioned and most of the people from that initial batch of migrants returned to China.

With the abolition of slavery, the need for new workers on the agricultural estates became critical. A second wave of Chinese immigration ensued. Most of these immigrants came from the southern Guangdong province. Between 1853 and 1866, the bulk of the immigrants that had arrived in Trinidad were hired as indentured labourers. At this time also, there were some free Chinese who migrated voluntarily in search of an improved way of life in the new world. The Chinese indentureship programme came to an end in 1866 as the Chinese and British governments could not agree upon terms of a comprehensive compensation package for the workers.

The Chinese revolution caused many Chinese to leave China. As a result, from 1911 to the mid-1940s, another influx of migrants arrived in Trinidad. During the years of the Chinese Revolution, foreign travel for most Chinese was very limited. It was not until around 1980 that degrees of freedom to travel from China were possible. These allowances have opened a portal for modern-day migration which is seen on a small scale at this present time.

Syrian and Lebanese Trinidadians and Tobagonians

At the turn of the twentieth century, Maronite Christians from Syria and Lebanon began to arrive in Trinidad. Many of them sought to immigrate to the 'New World' to make a new life. A few found themselves in Trinidad. They arrived at a time when the

economy was booming because of the strong cocoa and sugar markets in Continental Europe and England.

The migration to Trinidad by Syrian and Lebanese nationals was chiefly to escape political and religious persecution and economic hardship in their native countries. In those early years of migration, Syrians and Lebanese could only carry a suitcase with their immediate personal belongings. Their primary pursuit was to be part of a community free from social unrest.

In order to create an existence and a way of life in their new found home land of Trinidad, as new citizens, they were committed to becoming recognized as a significant part of the *Trinbagonian* national fabric. They brought with them vestiges of their culture and a keen business acumen which proved to be the ideal tools for success in the colony. Upon arriving in Trinidad and Tobago, they had little or no resources. However, with hard work and solidarity within their ranks, they eked out a thriving business niche in commerce, particularly in the textile and retail industries.

Mixed Trinidadians and Tobagonians

It is interesting to note that each group of people arriving at the comparatively small islands of Trinidad and Tobago, originated from countries of far greater landmass. However, these initially unrelated immigrant groups became geographically constrained to coexist in relatively closer proximity to each other. Sharing the same space has promoted a communal inclination to greater levels of social intermixing.

With constant close interaction, the inevitable interracial marriages and cohabitations have produced whole new breeds of people. Recent censuses show that at least 20% of the *Trinbagonian* population comprises persons of mixed race, a segment that is seen as the fastest growing demographic group. Notwithstanding, the accuracy of the real proportion of people of mixed races is difficult to determine. Census takers rely on information provided by people who self-report their ethnicity. There are many more people of mixed blood whose physical appearance manifests certain dominant ethnic traits above other latent characteristics. Sometimes being unaware of the full extent of one's true roots, a resignation to the outward visual manifestation often prevails.

An overall perspective of the people of this nation demonstrates that while some ethnic traits remain quite distinct and obvious, other characteristics are subtle and much less conspicuous. The ongoing cultural convergence of ethnicities continues to craft the consolidating identity of the people of this intriguing twin-island nation, Trinidad and Tobago - The land of a people with boundless pluralities and possibilities.

The enchanting beauty of women abounds in Trinidad and Tobago. Former Trinbagonian winners of global beauty pageants feature Janelle Penny Commissiong and Wendy Fitzwilliam, Miss Universe; and, Giselle Laronde, Miss World.

This skilled climber has no fear of heights as he cuts a bunch of coconuts

Fruit vendor - a common sight along the roads of Trinidad & Tobago

Roast corn vendor

Mayaro boys with brooms made from the freshly cut stalks from coconut branches

Football fans at the Hasley Crawford National Stadium

People & Culture - Sports

Trinbagonians are avid sports enthusiasts. Sports excite an almost delirious national passion. This exuberance is perhaps on greatest display during football (soccer) and cricket matches. In 2006, Trinidad and Tobago participated in the Football World Cup finals in Germany. Trinidad and Tobago was recognized as the smallest nation to have ever qualified for this most prestigious global sporting event. The team's involvement would only last through the preliminary group matches. However, the comparatively few Trinbagonian fans gained the accolade of being among the loudest with their supporting carnival-like cheers and accompanying pulsation from their rhythm-section drummers. Besides international soccer, Trinidad and Tobago also has contributed numerous players to major world club teams. Perhaps the most notable in this category is Tobagonian Dwight Yorke. This famous club player has won international admiration as a former prolific striker for the great Manchester United team in England.

Like football, the adulation for cricket is no less fervent. Internationally, Trinidad and Tobago cricket players combine in a confederation of other Caribbean players to form the West Indies Cricket Team. Trinidad and Tobago has given the world one of the greatest batsmen to have ever played the game – Brian Lara, the "Prince of Port of Spain." Lara holds several cricketing records, including the record for the highest individual score in first-class cricket for club team Warwickshire, with 501. He also remains listed as making the highest individual score in a test innings after scoring 400 not out for the West Indies against England in Antigua in 2004.

This diminutive twin-island state of Trinidad and Tobago has shone and continues to shine on the world stage beyond football and cricket. In recent years, Stephen Ames as a world-ranked winner on the famous US Professional Golf circuit won the Players Championship in 2006. The team of Trinbagonian ladies in the 1979 Netball Championship became illustrious world champions. At the 1976 Olympic Games in Montreal, Canada, Hasley Crawford was a world beater in winning gold at the 100 meter sprint finals. At the 2012 Games in London, Keshorn Walcott won the gold medal in the javelin field event, becoming the first athlete from the western hemisphere to win the competition in 60 years. Other carriers of the torch of glory in the arena of sports include Olympic medallists in track and field, Ato Bolden, Richard Thompson and Lalonde Gordon; and in swimming, George Bovell. A special recognition goes to the late Gizelle Salandy, who was ranked as the number one female light middleweight boxer of all-time in the world of boxing. Whilst her untimely passing has left a great void in women's boxing and the world of sports in general, she is fondly remembered as a champion's champion.

Winning and winning with style is a Trinbagonian passion!

Aranguez crab vendors enjoy a joke

Sumptuous curried crab sizzles in a pot

People & Culture - Foods

Delights, delicacies and dainties! As varied as the people of Trinidad and Tobago, so are the tastes in the foods that are favoured in typical *Trinbagonian* dining.

All of the usual international dishes are readily found at the range of fine restaurants and eateries around the nation. Resident local and international chefs make signature culinary statements with a Trinidad and Tobago accent to their dishes.

However, the soul of *Trinbagonian* cooking is best displayed in the 'Home Food' and 'Street Food' menus enjoyed by the locals. Traditional home cooking may include stewed chicken, rice and callaloo; pelau (also called 'one-pot' – featuring a variation of chicken, rice and beans combinations); curried crab and dumplings; fish broth and provision (potatoes, yams and dasheen); and, roti with curried chicken (sometimes alternated with beef, goat or shrimp), aloo (potatoes) and channa (chick peas). When on the streets, perhaps the most popular 'pick-up and go' item is doubles (a sandwich-like seasoned batter, fried and served with curried channa). There is also phulourie and chutney; corn on the cob - roasted or boiled; corn soup; and, souse a savory finger-food which can be made from pig, cow or chicken feet. It is seasoned in a spicy pickle of garlic, onion, salt, pepper, lemon and chadon beni.

Doubles and other East Indian delicacies on sale at Debe junction

When on the beach, especially at Maracas, 'bake and shark' is a must. A cool-down day at a river location is made complete with a famous 'curry duck' dish.

***Trinbagonian* flavors to savor!**

The French Creole and Spanish Flavours of Trinidad

The cultural impact made on society throughout Trinidad and Tobago can be said to be born out of much of the quality of life found in many small villages across the country's landscape. A good illustration of this is perhaps the little hill-side hamlet of Paramin. This seemingly unassuming rural locality is a significant contributor of important social ingredients to the bubbling mix of the national pot. Paramin features deep and far reaching roots in its inhabitants' racial origin, language, religion, food and even festive activities reflected across the country. The *raison d'être* behind the striking influences which this modest parish exerts can readily be ascribed to its colourful history. The molding of this community character bears the influential stamp of the colonial seal of the Spanish, and more significantly, the French, in the developing of this very distinct Caribbean twin-island state.

Under Spanish colonization, from 1498 when it was claimed by Christopher Columbus, Trinidad remained undeveloped until around 1783. By this time, the Spanish government of the day realized that to keep Trinidad as a viable colony, they needed to populate and develop the island. As a result, they crafted an initiative called the *Cedula of Population.* This scheme promoted an association with the neighbouring French colonists who shared the same Roman Catholic religious affinity as themselves. The plan offered ownership of land as an incentive to emigrate and settle in Trinidad. The principal beneficiaries of this deal were the white plantation owners and their African slaves, and French Creoles from Martinique. Additional migrants came from Guadeloupe, St. Lucia, Dominica, St. Martin, and to a lesser extent, Haiti. These new *émigrés* made huge contributions to the developing of the sugar industry which became the mainstay of the island's economy for many years. In 1787, *Mr. Picot de Lapeyrouse,* established the first sugar estate and factory in Trinidad. This rapidly increasing enterprise would attract even more settlers to Trinidad as a place to live and do business.

The island of Trinidad itself, though remaining sovereign to Spanish rule, became increasingly French in flavour and customs. Over time, more and more French settlers took up important administrative and social roles in the budding society. The predominant languages at this time were French and French Creole or *Kwèyòl*. The latter was spoken by the coloured and former African slaves from the colonies. The streets of Port-of-Spain, as well as towns and villages throughout the land began to grow with the influx of this new '*mezcla*', a mix of social liveliness and colour. This very dynamic nascent period in the cultural development of Trinidad and Tobago as a nation would become one of the primary pillars in the support of the superstructure of the national identity.

Out of this social convergence, a new breed of people known as Creoles began to emerge. The term Creole, derived from the Spanish word *criollo*, generally refers to people of local origin, whether black, white, or coloured. These persons would be the children of a racial mix who shared elements of a common culture impacted by African, Spanish, French, and English colonial influences.

With the passage of time and the advent of British capture and rule from 1797 onwards, Spanish, French and even Creole, gradually faded out as the dominant languages. From that era to the present time, English became the national language. As a legacy of the past however, there are a few districts where Creole, *Kwèyòl* or *Patois,* is still spoken. One of these villages is Paramin which also has elements of people who speak Spanish. Other settlements around Trinidad which demonstrate this Creole characteristic include such locations as Avocat, Blanchisseuse, Bourg Mulatresse, Brasso Seco, La Croix, La Lune, Morne, and Toco. Like Paramin, these villages are places where the early French planters who came to Trinidad secured land and chose to settle. Many in these communities still retain traces of their ancestral heritage.

Beside the established French Creole flavor in the land, another notable addition to the cultural blend is represented by the people called '*cocoa panyols*'. This group is made up of descendants of Amerindian, Spanish and African ancestors, a distinct hybrid of ethnicities whose formative roots were developed in Venezuela, who add a particularly colourful dimension to the Trinidadian social complex. In the 19th and early 20th centuries, this Spanish speaking group of people were attracted to Trinidad to come and work on the great cocoa estates which were primarily situated across the country's Northern and Central Ranges. As they worked in these estates, they formed and maintained tight-knit communities in the isolated valleys of these hillside regions

Gardeners tending lush Paramin vegetables

closely preserving many of their distinct set of cultural practices. Like the Coloured French Creoles, the Cocoa Panyols added another dimension to the ethnic and social mix of the country characterized by their physical appearance, language, food, dance and style of dress.

The village of Paramin ranks highly as a single location which provides a fascinating insight into the many and varied social nuances which describe Trinidad and Tobago. For most of the year, the people of Paramin are quietly engaged in its main activity of agriculture. However, there are three days in the year when Paramin comes to life and draws national attention. Firstly, on the second Sunday in November each year, residents celebrate the harvest season. People gather and indulge in games, music, and traditional feasting on 'wildmeat' including agouti, deer, lappe, tattoo, and wild hog. Secondly, on the Monday before Christmas, Paramin hosts its famous *'parang' festival.* Parang features bands of singers singing lively and energetic Spanish songs accompanied by rhythmic music which is enjoyed all around Trinidad and Tobago throughout the Christmas season. Thirdly, on Carnival Monday, two days before the beginning of the Lenten season, Paramin becomes the home of the famed *'blue devil'* masqueraders who paint and cover themselves in a greasy blue dye and powder. These devilish performers take to the streets with a freedom of unrestrained festive revelry. It is also noteworthy that at Paramin's Catholic Church, *Our Lady of Guadeloupe*, on each Sunday before Carnival, *Dimanche Gras*, there is a time-honoured tradition of conducting the entire mass of that day in Creole as a liturgical celebration of the community's past.

Paramin exudes an abundance of flavors. Indeed, from a culinary perspective, there are many local dishes in Trinidad and Tobago which are influenced by the savory garden produce grown in this little village which some call the nation's herbs and seasonings capital. A veritably fertile community famous for its prime herbs and vegetables which include huge chive, parsley, peppers, thyme, tomatoes, cabbage and a remarkable variety of other aromatic plants including the locally famed chadon-beni, also known by its Hindi name, bhandhania, a very pungent plant used in seasoning that gives a distinctly Trinbagonian flavor. Generations of the resident hill-side dwellers have perfected the farming techniques which now deliver herbs and seasonings favoured by the chefs of some of the country's finest restaurants. Also, many of the country's markets are supplied with an extensive variety of products from this renowned gardening region perched on the north-western slopes of the great northern range.

Located in the north of Trinidad between the towns of Maraval and Diego Martin, Paramin sits high in the hills above the city of Port-of-Spain. The cool hill-side elevations are often

Breathtaking views from Paramin

Spanish Thyme

shrouded in a seemingly mystical wafting mist, creating a distinctive atmosphere that is particularly conducive to the superlative growth of the prime crops for which it is known.

Access into this cozy village cannot be easily made by a casual stroll. It requires the use of a sturdy 4-wheel-drive vehicle to ascend the precipitous and uneven concrete Paramin Road which climbs and zigzags northward and upward. It rises sharply through the steep incline to the summit of its location. It is nestled in the undulating lushness of the verdant Northern Range where it overlooks the Caribbean Sea to the north. From these heights, there are breathtaking views of the entire northwestern promontory of the island. Distant views of the islands of the Dragon's Mouth are visible to the west, and the Gulf of Paria to the south, with extraordinary vistas of the coasts of the Caroni Swamp. On a clear day, the panorama extends further to the industrial city of San Fernando and even to the South American coast of Venezuela beyond.

Paramin is like a little time-capsule containing key features of the past. This small village provides an array of unique cultural ingredients which define the inimitable social character and flavor of Trinidad and Tobago.

Northern Range view of Maracas Valley, St. Joseph and beyond

Nature has a way of painting its own canvas as seen in this sunset at Store Bay, Tobago

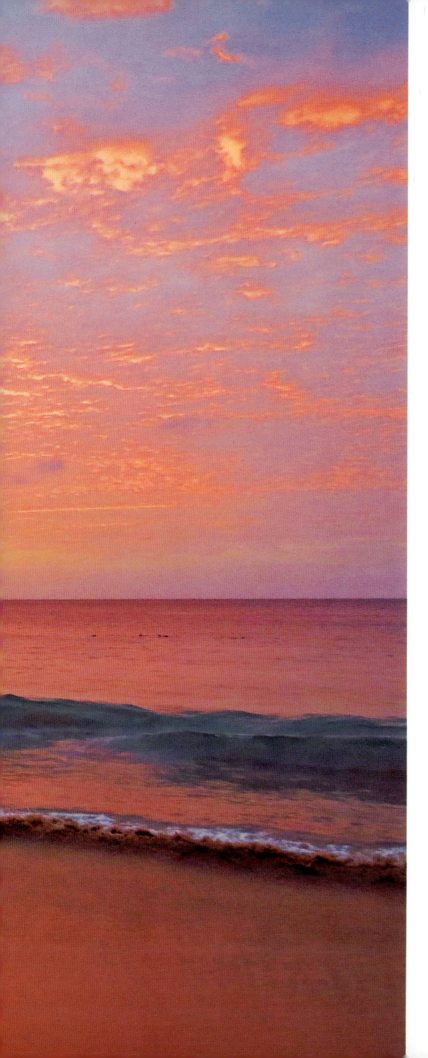

Tobago - the Mystique of its Beauty

In the midst of all the usual tropical trappings and splendour of sun, sea and sand, the tiny island of Tobago distinguishes itself as not just another typical Caribbean island.

Ambling around Tobago one will encounter exotic places like Les Coteaux, Courland, Glamorgan, La Guira, Lampsins Bay and Mesopotamia. There are also famous historical battlements including Fort Monck, French Fort and Fort King George which stand out as great coastal features. Relics of sprawling sugar mills and water wheels testify to a range of once thriving plantations of bygone western European colonial enterprise. At virtually every turn there is an odd mix of different foreign names and terms which abound like nowhere else in the region. The very name of the island, 'Tobago,' tells of a culture which predates the entry of Europeans. This complex of languages provokes a certain sense of: Where did all these titles come from? Who were the people responsible for these labels? Under what circumstances did they come into being? In the meantime, and perhaps whilst quizzically trying to connect the dots of why there is such a profusion of varied languages in such a small geographic area, a very curious Tobagonian tradition leaps forward as a very distracting attraction – Goat Racing! At the small south western village of Buccoo, the almost defying spectacle of barefoot 'jockeys', kitted out in their racing colours with starting gate numbers on their jerseys, sprint behind their 'rides' holding them at the end of long reins of rope. The wonderment of a shouting gallery cheering on their preferred racers is virtually transfixing whilst both goats and jockeys frenetically gallop to the finish line. If still enthused for more unusual racing excitement, there is also 'crab races' – nimble land crustaceans pitted against each other scurrying along a contrived course whilst being prodded by sticks!

Yes! Tobago is definitely one of the most intriguing and endearing locations throughout the entire Caribbean. This 300 km2 sister-isle of Trinidad, with a population of approximately 50,000 people, is as much a part of, as it is apart from, its larger national relative. At the south-eastern corner of the Caribbean Sea at a point adjacent to the Atlantic Ocean, these two diminutive sibling landmasses meet and co-exist. They are separated by just twenty-two miles of tropical seas, a geographical divide which, in many ways, has contributed to the distinct historical developments which have significantly defined their similar yet different cultural identities.

Kids from the fishing village of Black Rock, Tobago, enjoy an early morning catch

Goat racing in Buccoo and Mount Pleasant is a celebrated event in Tobago during Easter weekends

Tobago today reflects a history that has recognized it as one of the most treasured and sought after prizes of the Caribbean. This virtue is highlighted by the fact that more nations have fought for the possession of this tropical jewel than for any other island in the entire region. Long before the arrival of the Europeans, the then resident Carib Indians had great clashes with other Amerindian tribes from the South American mainland. They battled each other intensely to retain this haven which they called 'Tavaco' the place of their favoured plant (modern-day tobacco) used for smoking. After Christopher Columbus' sighting in 1498, then from around the late 1500's to the early 1600's, the indigenous people had to confront interests from further afield. They now faced fleets of invading European colonists against whom they bravely resisted but eventually succumbed.

Its prime location strategically positioned on the developing shipping routes to other Lesser Antillean islands and the South American mainland made Tobago a sort of 'Look Out' in the Southern Caribbean. As contending European nations sought to capitalize on the benefits this gateway island offered, subsequent years featured great tug-of-war encounters chiefly between the Spanish, Courlanders (Latvians), Dutch, English, French and others as they frequently and relentlessly battled each other for claim of this trophy of the Caribbean. As a result of these numerous conflicts, the governing of the island changed over thirty times. Finally, in 1814, the British prevailed in their quest for colonial rule under the Treaty of Paris. Seventy-five years later, in 1889, Tobago was linked with Trinidad to form a single British colony. In 1962, as a twin-island nation, Trinidad and Tobago gained independence from the British, and later in 1976, became a republic.

The rich legacy of Tobago's colourful past is now firmly in the hands of present-day Tobagonians. Generations of Tobagonians have evolved from the days of colonial rule when sugar, cotton and indigo plantations were being established and thousands of Africans were brought to the island for slave labour. Unlike Trinidad, the people of Tobago have largely remained homogeneous, consisting of people mainly of African descent. It is evident that Tobagonians are hugely proud of their heritage. A sense of intense nationalism is displayed through a character and lifestyle that has its roots in a network of village life. It is a way of life that is somewhat akin to the age-old rural West African village model in which the individual and the whole are developed through cooperative effort for the good of all. As a local Tobagonian expression, this communal practice is familiarly called 'len han'.

As Tobago's history has shown when external forces sought to dispossess previous occupants in the land, there is

The traditional Moriah Wedding in Moriah is a central part of the Tobago Heritage Festival

A wedding gift bearer

This couple dances the 'Tobago Jig', a dance originally performed by the British colonist

Dancing the Cocoa in Charlotteville

Colourful sun umbrellas line the beach at Store Bay

expressive in all they do, perhaps in none more so than in the performances at the many exhibitions celebrating their culture and heritage. These portrayals can be seen during the many festivals which commemorate traditions that have a strong African influence. Cultural events include musical and dance performances of Bèlé (or Bel Air), Reel and Jig, and Speech Bands – the keepers of Tobago's oral tradition. In the village of Moriah, the most famous rendition of the 'Ole time Tobago Wedding' is enacted. The entire show includes a procession of the bride and groom, wedding guests and gift bearers, all accompanied by the merriment and music of the 'fiddle and tamb'rin'. The question may arise as to how Tobagonians maintain the seemingly unending energy levels exhibited in their passionate performances. Perhaps it is fuelled by some of their typical everyday food staples. The famed curried crab and dumplings, and Tobago Blue Food (dasheen - ground tuber) dishes are great favourites. For those with a sweet tooth, there are béné balls (sesame seed brittle-candy) and toolum (grated coconut and molasses confectionery). And for that particular extra 'get-up-and-go' boost, a drink of the legendary pacro water (an elixir made from local shellfish) to spark new zeal. Tobagonians take great pride in their cultural past. They ensure its preservation through to later generations by story-telling, folk tales, superstitions and morality plays.

now a recurrence in the form of a contemporary foreign adversary which seeks to lay hold of this precious land. The invasion of modern influences seems intent to captivate and erode many core Tobagonian social values and traditions. However, there is a repelling fortress-like resilience within the Tobagonian character present in villages like Charlotteville, Castara, Delaford, L'Anse Fourmi, Parlatuvier, Speyside and across the land where there is a tenacious hold on safeguarding that almost indelible nature, the inherent charisma that is exclusively Tobagonian. This very determined self-preserving mission extends to the local governing of Tobago which is exercised through the chambers of the Tobago House of Assembly. It is a devolved entity within the central government of Trinidad and Tobago with a legal mandate aimed at, "making better provision for the administration of the island of Tobago and for matters therewith."

Hard working and hard playing, there is a great passion for life that illustrates the Tobagonian way. The people are intensely

Fittingly, Tobago's verdant landscape and natural habitat serve as an ideal backdrop in support of the luxuriant atmosphere found the length and breadth of this quite alluring island. In the approximately twenty-one miles long and seven miles wide land area, there are tropical rain forests, numerous coves and bays with tranquil beaches of pristine white sand. There are crystalline waterfalls, streams and rivers emanating from the highlands. At various locations along the coast-line there are mangroves, swamps and lagoons which form elaborate eco-system complexes. Wild life is particularly varied and flourishing with mammals, bats, frogs, lizards, marine turtles, snakes and butterflies. The species of birds are spectacular; they include the red-billed tropicbird, rufous-tailed jacamar, blue-crowned motmot, and the cocrico – this latter being a tropical pheasant that is native to Tobago, and with the scarlet ibis, is recognized as one of the national birds of Trinidad and Tobago.

Tobago remains as much sought-after today as its history testifies. Tobagonians and visitors alike are enticed to capture and keep a piece of this Caribbean jewel. It can therefore be understood why Columbus' first glimpse of this unusually picturesque island would have been so engaging and enchanting. His descriptive name, 'La Bella Forma' was a clear recognition to the attraction of – The Mystique of its Beauty!

Enjoying the crystal clear waters of Pigeon Point

Windsurfing off the lower end of Pigeon Point

From Store Bay to Charlotteville - Two ends of paradise in Tobago

Store Bay, Tobago

Charlotteville, Tobago

HOMESTEAD
...In the fervour of my song,
I hold him firm upon the fields
In many homely images,
His ghost's as tall as the tall trees:
He tramps these tracks his business made
By daily roundabout in boots,
Tougher and earthier than roots;
And every furrow of the earth
And every wind-blown blade of grass
Knows him the spirit of the place.

By Tobagonian Poet,
Eric Merton Roach (1915-1974)

Lighthouse and cannon at Fort George overlooking the capital of Scarborough

African Folk Dance

When travelling around Trinidad and Tobago it quickly becomes evident that dance and music are central components in the cultural expression of the people. Predominantly manifest, are the various strains of African dance and rhythms which permeate virtually all other musical genres here. This influential art-form has its roots primarily in West Africa, the region from which most people of African descent in the Caribbean originated. As in the mother land, dance and music play a very important role in just about all aspects of the lives of most Trinbagonians. This art-form can be displayed at births, weddings, celebrations, festivals, deaths and religious rituals. The sound of music and the corresponding sway of the body is ever audible and visible.

African dance is typically expressed through multiple rhythmic movements engaging a total body expression. Shoulders, chest, pelvis, arms, and legs seemingly synchronize with different rhythms in the music. The dancer may also add rhythmic components as if they were extensions to the instrumental music created by the music of the body. The result is a complex harmony of body and music which accomplishes an amazing sensory expression.

In Trinidad and Tobago, many African folk dances remain and are even embellished through new and evolving cultural influences. The traditional music that accompanies folk dances is mainly the African drum. Folk dance in Trinidad and Tobago is rich and varied. Some of the more popular dance forms include:

Bèlé or Bel Air - A passionately expressive celebratory and social dance originally found among the African/French (Creoles slaves) in Haiti, Martinique, and other islands.

Canboulay - A colourful re-enactment march through the streets, depicting what actually took place on estates when the sugar cane fields were being burned prior to harvest to remove trash and insects. The name comes from the French "cannes brulee", burning of the sugar canes.

Kalinda – A dance or game performed as fighting with sticks.

Limbo - This dance form, also known as the 'Under the Stick Dance', is readily perceived as a general Caribbean feature. However, the evolution of limbo can be specifically attributed to Trinidad and Tobago. The thumping beats of the drum is the usual form of musical accompaniment. In a rhythmic movement, the dancer leans backward to dance and travel under a pole. If the dancer touches the pole or falls backwards to the floor, the dancer withdraws, and others continue. The pole is typically lowered until only one dancer can make it under the stick without touching it or falling.

Folklore surrounding limbo dancing in Trinidad and Tobago suggests that the movements of this dance represent the cycle of life. When the dancer moves under the stick and emerges at the other side, the clearing of the pole symbolises the triumph of life over death. Traditional limbo dancing was a ritual originally performed at 'wakes', as a funeral dance which perhaps related to the African legba or legua dance.

Orisha/Shango – Religious dance performed or depicted by Shango observers, originating from the West African Yoruba ritual systems.

Pique - A more erotic version of the Bèlé or Bel Air performed with great flair and accented hip movements.

Dance performance from Best Village cultural festival

How low can you go? This is Limbo, a national dance of Trinidad and Tobago

Odissi dancers in a reflective posture outside the Hyatt Regency Hotel in Port of Spain

East Indian Cultural Dance

The wonderfully exotic presentations of East Indian dance, as seen in Trinidad and Tobago, represent a fundamentally inborn element in the culture of people of East Indian descent. Though generations removed from the land of their forefathers, dance for this Trinbagonian ethnic group is a very important practice in their cultural self-expression. With as much emphasis as given to religion, language, songs, food or other rituals, these time-honoured silky body movements, which so identify that distinct East Indian characteristic, have been keenly preserved in a geographical setting far away from their origins.

East Indian dance forms can range from the very demure and graceful to the very elaborate and frenetic. All the various dance styles can be chiefly organized into three main groups: classical, folk and modern. Classical Indian dance dates back several centuries. These dance patterns were usually practiced in the royal courts and temples. Folk dancing tended to be developed more in the rural areas as expressions of daily work and the rituals of village life. Modern East Indian dance is a creative mixture of the first two forms, combining liberally improvised movements and rhythms to express the new themes and impulses of present-day life.

The basis of East Indian dance was developed as a set of integral activities in religious rituals. During these events, dancers worshipped the gods by telling stories about the varied circumstances of life's occurrences. There are principally three primary components which form the foundation of these dances. They are natya, the dramatic element of the dance, i.e., the imitation of character traits and behaviour. Secondly, nritta, a pure dance in which the rhythms and lyrics of the music are reflected in the decorative movements of the hands and body along with the stamping of the feet; and finally, nritya, the portrayal of mood through facial expression, hand gesture, and various feet positions. Examples of these dance forms derived from the eight principal classical dances include:

Bharata Natyam - Originating from the Tamil Nadu region of South India, this dance is recognized as one of the oldest East Indian dance-styles. The principles of this dance are based on the Natya Shastra, a comprehensive treatise on Indian dramaturgy. Performances of the Bharata Natyam were originally danced in temples by the Devadasis, the servants of gods and goddesses. The movements of this dance are based on pure rhythmical elements, conveying a language of hand-gestures and facial expressions.

Kathak – Originating out of the region of Uttar Pradesh in northern India, this dance can be traced back to the nomadic singers and musicians known as Kathaks, or storytellers, in ancient times. Kathak presentations have elements of temple and ritual dances. The dancer dances with two hundred ghungroos, bells on the feet, to the musical accompaniments of the sarangi and tabla. This dance form is executed with smooth gliding movements. A primary posture of the dancer is to maintain a straight back while holding one arm vertically and the other extended at shoulder height. With the torso remaining still, the dancer performs fast-paced dance steps.

Odissi – Also known as Orissi, originated from the state of Orissa, in eastern India. It is distinguished from other dance forms by the importance it places upon the Tribhangi, meaning the three part break. These are seen in the independent movements of the head, chest and pelvis. This dance is also characterized by various Bhangas, standing positions, which involve stamping of the foot and striking various postures as seen in Indian sculptures. Considered both a classical and devotional dance form, Odissi portrays a distinct feminine sensuality with an air of enticing sophistication.

Kuchipudi – This is a lively and rhythmic dance ascribed to Andhra Pradesh in South East India. The evolution of this dance is particularly marked by the influence of Siddhendra Yogi. Similar to the Bharata Natyam, this dance also emphasizes rhythmical elements of hand gestures and facial expressions.

Ghatka – Of Punjabi origin, this is a dance of celebration which has evolved as an expression usually performed at weddings and other festive occasions. Traditionally, two men, each holding colourful sticks, would dance around each other and joust or tap their sticks together in rhythm with the music of accompanying drums. This dance imitates the olden Sikh martial art practice in the skilful use of swords, sticks, and daggers.

Jharoo – This dance also called the Broom dance is typically performed by up to twelve persons, each carrying cocoyea (the woody shaft of the leaves from a coconut tree branch) brooms known as jharoos in either hand. Participants dance around in circles, in weaving motions between each other with turns. They sing and maintain a steady rhythm which is punctuated by hitting their own jharoo together at intervals. At certain points, they meet and strike each other's jharoos and then bend and strike the ground. They can then change their formation and dance in pairs, with one circling the other whilst they both continue striking their brooms to the dance rhythm.

Kollatam - This is a dance in which two kolas (a kola is a stick which is about an arms-length) are used for producing rhythmic sounds while in motion. The choreography and rhythm structure vary slightly from that of the Jharoo and the effort is somewhat more vigorous in its actions. Beautiful songs and chants and traditional instruments consisting of special drums, tablas, accordions, and hand cymbals are used to accompany the dancers. Both men and women participate in the Kollatam. During a performance the participants sing songs and move while they beat the two sticks. This art form requires a team of ten or twelve participants. The costumes are very colourful with the girls wearing long skirts, short sleeved blouses and orhinis (head veils). The boys sometimes wear the traditional wraps called dhotis with hip length shirts or more conventional wear.

A central theme consistent in East Indian dance is that of dealing with the emotions and feelings of humankind through the expressions of love, hatred, anger and jealousy. The presentations of these dances often portray the eternal quest of humankind to unify the soul with the divine one.

In Trinidad and Tobago, custodians of the East Indian traditional art-form do earnestly strive to safeguard the identity of the indigenous oriental Indian dance styles and movements. However, with the advent of new local music and dance expressions such as Chutney, there is a distinct Caribbean evolution to conventional East Indian dance. East Indian dance in the Islands, whilst remaining true to its core principles, incorporates and blends an array of vibrant rhythms taken from the broad diversity of other resident contemporary cultures. Consequently, this dance-form, as performed in Trinidad and Tobago, is an evolution and a unique representation of the original and typical dances of the Sub-Continent.

Satnarine Balkaransingh performs a Kathak dance in his show 'Rang Tarang' at the Little Carib Theatre

The element of fire is depicted in Nrityanjali's production 'Shiva the Cosmic Dancer' performed at Queen's Hall, Port of Spain

The Scarf Dance - Dancers of the Nrityanjali Theatre perform a Folk Rumal

Nrityanjali's production of 'Dasavatar' depicting Sita sitting under the tree guarded by Ravana's soldier. Performed at Queen's Hall, Port of Spain

Multi-cultural & Contemporary Dance

A Metamorphosis School of Dance presentation - One of the top contemporary dance schools in Trinidad and Tobago

Waltz of the Dancing Princesses by the Cascade Festival Ballet.

Nalini Akal performs this Middle Eastern dance

Metamorphosis school of dance

The Drums of Trinidad and Tobago

In virtually every social or cultural event in Trinidad and Tobago where music is an integral element, the beat of the drum is ever present and distinct. From religious to secular functions, tvaried percussive are a familiar staple.

The role of the drum in the culture of Trinidad and Tobago is as important to the various resident ethnic groups as it is anywhere else in world. The reverberating sounds of the drum seem to dictate the rhythm and pace by which many day-to-day activities are conducted. From what may be a sombre monotone to that of a pulsating orchestration, the drum, in many ways, echoes the heartbeat and mood of the nation.

Throughout Trinidad and Tobago one can find numerous kinds of percussive instruments. They range from the traditionally recognizable skin covered drum, to unlikely improvised pieces of metal objects. A drum may even take an imaginary form. At a whim, any make-shift surface can be instantly transformed into the would-be drummer's immediate instrumental demand. It is no wonder therefore, that striking up a resounding rhythm requires little prompting for the typically spontaneous *Trinbagonian* who seems ever ready to never miss a beat.

It can be said that for all the people of Trinidad and Tobago, from a lesser to a greater degree, whether African, Anglo, Amerindian, Chinese, French, Indian, Lebanese, Portuguese, Spanish, Syrian, or any of the resident ethnic combinations, there is an inherent inclination to the sound of the drum. As a consequence, the various forms of drums present in the national culture are abundant and as assorted as the people themselves. Here is a selection of some of the drums found in this land of music:

Baydum - Double-headed bass drum used in *Hosay* (*Hosein*) rituals, now also widespread among *Afro-Trinbagonians* and others.

Bemba - *Cylindrical drums with double skins; smallest of the set with conga and oumalay drums.*

Boula - Double-headed barrel drum, played open handed. Drum heads are attached with hoops, accompany *kalinda* stick fighting.

Claves *(Toc-Toc)* – A instrument consisting of a pair of short sections of wood, like rosewood or ebony . When struck together they produce a bright clicking noise. Claves are sometimes hollow and carved in the middle to amplify the sound.

Cutter - Single-headed barrel drum, played open handed; drum heads attached with hoops. Popular accompaniment for *kalinda* stick fighting.

Dhantal – The Dhantal is an instrument originally created by East Indians during their period of indentured labour on the sugar estates of old. The dhantal is a long steel rod adapted from the prong used to connect the yokes of the bullocks that transported the sugarcane on the plantations. The metal horse shoes used on the estate horses and mules were used to strike the *dhantal* to provide rhythmic sound.

Dholak - Traditional Indian double-headed hand-drum played from both sides.

Djemba - Of West African origin, this is a skin-covered hand drum shaped like a large goblet meant to be played with bare hands.

Güiro *(scratcher)* - An open-ended hollow gourd with parallel notches cut in one side. It is played by rubbing a wooden stick along the notches to produce a ratchet-like sound.

Iron - Primarily the brake iron from a car's wheel. Other metal objects may substitute.

Oumalay - Cylindrical drums with double skins, middle-sized drum of the set with *bembe* and *conga* drums.

Tamboo Bamboo - Hollowed out sections of bamboo cut to different lengths. Percussive sounds are made by pounding the longer lengths of bamboo against the ground. The shorter lengths are hand-held and struck with a mallet.

Tassa - Kettle drum with a goatskin head, used in various East Indian festivities.

Tumba - Tall, narrow, single-headed drum of the set with *bembe* and *oumalay* drums

Whilst all these may be champions of the percussive sound in their own right, chief among the drums of Trinidad and Tobago is the national instrument, the 'steel pan.' It is recognized as the only musical instrument to have been invented in the 20th century. The steel pan was formally created in the 1930's, but its rich history can be traced back through a circuitous chain of events to the enslaved Africans who were brought to the islands during the late 1700's. The loud and even thunderous sounds of the beat of African drums on festive occasions began to be seen as inciting and seditious by the British authorities of the day. As a result, the colonial masters enforced a rigid ban against the playing of the traditional drum. Undeterred by this intolerant legal action, the creative instincts of the people ensured that the voice of the drum would not be silenced. They sought alternate objects, besides the traditional hand-drum, to create that familiar throbbing sound, the necessary accompaniment to their natural inborn rhythm. These items included bamboo tubes, scrap metal parts, metal graters and even dustbin lids. Out of this inventive defiance and the quest to preserve the sanctity of their personal identity, the 'steel pan' would be born.

This remarkable invention was the product of a few seemingly unassuming men from a district called Laventille, in the eastern region of the city of Port of Spain. In the minds of the uninformed, it was a locality considered to be a socially challenged ghetto. In fact, it proved to be a seat of world-beating innovation. These men took discarded fifty-five gallon metal drums which were originally used as storage containers for petroleum and transformed them into remarkable musical instruments. Through a series of experimentations by heating and pounding on the base of the drums, they created hollowed concave surfaces across which they further chiselled contoured convex panels which were then tuned into the full range of musical notes.

A certain corresponding set of circumstances may well be drawn between the creation of the national instrument and the development of the nation of Trinidad and Tobago. Through a series of constraining and fated societal issues of the day, and being made subject to a phase and process of constant hammering and tempering, a unique and vibrant culture was moulded and pressed into existence.

Led by renowned steel-pan arranger, Len 'Boogsie' Sharpe, Phase-II Pan Groove steel orchestra performs at the Panorama finals

Two Kings and a Queen! The King of Calypso, the Mighty Sparrow, and the Queen of Calypso, Calypso Rose, stand on either side of the King of Soca, Machel Montano

Ravi B is a past winner of the national Chutney Soca competition

Calypso, Soca & Chutney Music in Trinidad and Tobago

Trinidad and Tobago is the home of calypso, the rhythmic sound of Caribbean island music. Throughout the land, the air is perpetually filled with tuneful harmonies which seem to accompany every moment. Calypso is a distinct feature in the character of the people of this colourful twin-island nation.

Trinbagonians are expressive to the point of an exhibition, whether physically or vocally. Life seems always to be conducted through the vehicle of a performance. The calypso singer is the embodiment of the social character of the nation. The calypsonian takes to the stage with melodic verses and lyrical *'picong'*, which is satire and derision, or even praise. Spontaneously and extemporaneously, the calypsonian expresses the pulse of the nation. The beat may be racy or calm, but always a tuneful social commentary of life, love and the politics of it all!

Passionate fans wave their flags and rags at the Soca Monarch finals on Carnival Friday

Calypso as an art-form is accepted as the national folk song of Trinidad and Tobago. The roots of calypso, or *kaiso* as it is sometimes termed, are deep within the African lore of the nation. Its prominence began in the era of the emancipation of the slaves. Those nascent *Trinbagonians* preserved the historical threads of song and music from their West African tribal ancestors. They intertwined this ancient musical tapestry into their early songs which were the forerunners of the modern-day calypso.

Many of the traditional calypsonians are known by sobriquets. Famous singers of old include the Mighty Bomber, Growling Tiger, Lord Kitchener and the Mighty Duke. Present legends include the Mighty Sparrow, Calypso Rose, Black Stalin, Singing Francine, Shadow, David Rudder, Lord Nelson and Lord Superior. All these are considered giants in the field of calypso music. They have all taken the genre to new and elevated levels. However, as a living organism, calypso has evolved. Whilst retaining its traditional constructs, it has derived the popular off-shoot called *Soca*. This new form is essentially a blend of Soul and Calypso music. *Soca* is most enjoyed among the youth and is championed by such musical luminaries as Machel Montano, Ras Shortie (deceased), Super Blue, Iwer George, Kes Dieffenthaler, Shurwayne Winchester, Bunji Garlin, Fayanne Alvarez, Patrice Roberts and Destra Garcia.

The mechanics in the evolution of calypso music have also impacted the progress of other indigenous music in the same way. The progress of Chutney music, deriving from its traditional East Indian cultural roots, bears certain similarities to that of the relationship between *Soca* and Calypso. Chutney music in its own right has also gained great levels of appeal, particularly among the young people of East Indian descent in Trinidad and Tobago. Popular chutney artistes include Sundar Popo, Sonny Mann, Ricky Jai, Drupatee, Ravi B and KI.

The singing artistes fill the airways with an eclectic range of compositions. Their renditions are greatly anticipated and appreciated. The masses revel in those songs which tell the stories of their every-day life's activities. The people are excited and demand an encore for: **Kaiso, Kaiso, Kaiso!**

Elevation of the National Academy of the Performing Arts (NAPA) in Port of Spain

Architecture
& Monuments

The physical legacy of a nation's cultural heritage is seen in its architecture and monuments.

The landscape of Trinidad and Tobago has been adorned with numerous monuments and structures. Many of these buildings have become recognized and prized as unique national symbols with each representing certain aspects of local life.

A review of the array of the nation's architecture and monuments readily gives an insight into the stark and lively design intents of the nation's past and present architects and artisans. From earlier centuries to current times, the variety of existing structures gives pause for perspective. There are replicas of ancient edifices representing an era distinguished by Amerindian habitats. There is a bridge to the present age which is replete with colonial facades, battlements of cannons and coastal lighthouses. There are great religious structures. Additionally, there are sculpted monuments of past heroes, artistic impressions, and curiously wrought promenades. New skylines now feature the glistening glass and steel of ultra modern city skyscrapers. All these structures are milestones of design across the national landscape. They stand as pillars of architectural traditions that have influenced the course of life on these islands.

Some classic and extraordinary local craftsmanship are represented with constructions ranging from the dominant and imposing to the demure and non-descript. They include:

The Red House in Port of Spain, which houses the nation's Parliament, the seat of the government of Trinidad and Tobago.

The Roman Catholic **Cathedral of the Immaculate Conception** in Port of Spain.

The Anglican **Holy Trinity Cathedral** in Port of Spain.

The Magnificent Seven are a famous group of mansions located in the Queen's Park Savannah area in the city of Port of Spain. These wonderful period buildings of colonial grandeur are: **Stollmeyer's Castle, Whitehall, Archbishop's House, Roomor, Mille Fleurs, Hayes Court, and Queen's Royal College.**

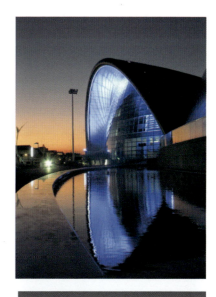

The Benedictine Monastery at **Mount St. Benedict** nestled in the hillsides of the towering Northern Range.

...Positively engaging and enthralling. Sites truly to behold!

Dotted around the countryside of both Trinidad and Tobago, one can still find relics of *ajoopas*, little rickety wooden buildings, weather-beaten and scarred with the passage of time. These structures were the olden homes of African and East Indian workers on the plantations of rice, sugarcane, cocoa and other crops.

The Hindu culture is represented by many sites including the marvellous **Temple in the Sea** at

Water Fountain at Woodford Square, Port of Spain

Waterloo. There is also the towering and statuesque **Hanuman Monument** at Carapichaima. It is the largest statue of the Hindu monkey god, outside of India.

Modern architecture boasts the sprawling splendour of the **National Academy of the Performing Arts** at Queen's Park Savannah in Port of Spain and its equally attractive sister-building in the southern city of San Fernando.

The gleaming modern commercial complex comprising government buildings and the Hyatt Regency Hotel fashioned as an art deco waterfront feature near the port of Port of Spain.

The constructed environment in Trinidad and Tobago abounds with a vast range of architectural styles. Whether public structures or private dwellings, these are landmark memorials which are enshrined as physical legacies of the nation's heritage.

...Positively engaging and enthralling. Sites truly to behold!

The Renaissance Towers, Glencoe, Port of Spain

Waterfront buildings at the port of Port of Spain

National Library and Information Services Building—Rotunda at spiralling staircase beneath skylight; Port of Spain

One of the 'Magnificent 7' colonial buildings at Queen's Park Savannah, Port of Spin, Queen's Royal College is the oldest secondary school in Trinidad and Tobago. The architecture of the building is German Renaissance in style.

Nature Preserve House, Tobago

The Great House of Charles Joseph, Count de Loppinot (1738–1819), is situated in the village which carries his name, Lopinot. This splendid colonial house was once part of Loppinot's cocoa estate, La Reconnaissance, nestled in the foothills on the northern range and about five miles north of the town of Arouca.

The Lion House, a memorial to the indentured East Indian immigrants who came to Trinidad starting from 1845, is located on the Main Road in Chaguanas. Now also famously known as, 'A House for Mr. Biswas', in the novel of that title written by Trinidad and Tobago's Nobel Laureate for literature, Sir Vidia S. Naipaul.

The Red House, Port of Spain

Colonial Government
Houses of Colour

Statements of colour are everywhere in Trinidad and Tobago. Among the varied national expressions in tones and hues, two very prominent buildings in the nation's capital city of Port of Spain majestically declare their place in the spectrum - *The Red House* and *Whitehall*. These two sites not only display an appearance of eye catching tint and shade, but project a sense of ostentatious architectural charisma. They invoke the grandeur of a bygone European era of building designs as landmark portraits in a tropical setting which command visual attention.

Located in the heart of the city, the impressive structure of the *Red House* accommodates the nation's government, the Parliament of Trinidad and Tobago. The building was first called, the *Red House*, in 1897 when Trinidad and the entire British Commonwealth were preparing to celebrate the Diamond Jubilee of Queen Victoria. As a special commemorative gesture, the building was painted in a lustrous red which prompted people to call it *'The Red House'* because of its new colour.

From early Colonial times, the affairs of government for the nation have always been carried out in buildings at the site of the *Red House*. Two previous structures occupying this location were totally destroyed by devastating outbreaks of fire in the city of Port of Spain in respective episodes of 1808 and 1903. The rebuilding work of 1904 to 1907 produced the resplendent structure which has remained as it is seen to this day.

Located along Maraval Road, opposite the Queen's Park Savannah in Port of Spain, the sumptuous property called *Whitehall* is distinctly recognisable among many of the other featured structures in the vicinity. This beautiful building was erected in 1904 by Joseph Leon Agostini, a wealthy cocoa planter and entrepreneur. Soon after construction, Agostini died and his wife sold the property to Mr. Robert Henderson, an American businessman from Venezuela. Henderson would subsequently name the building *'Whitehall'* after the white coral limestone that was used in its construction. Built by the Barbadian builder, James Moore, the distinct architectural design of *Whitehall* is a Moorish Mediterranean style found in Corsica where the Agostini family originated.

Initially a private family residence, Whitehall would become a key administrative and governmental office over the years. From 1940, these premises were commandeered by United States Armed Forces in Trinidad during World War II. In 1944, the British Council rented and occupied the building as a cultural center. The Trinidad Central Library, the Regional Library, the National Archives, the Government Broadcasting Unit, the Trinidad Art Society and the Cellar Club all rented or occupied

Whitehall, Port of Spain

space in the building. In 1949, the lease to the British Council was not renewed and the building remained empty until the 7 October, 1954, when it was purchased by the Government of Trinidad and Tobago. In 1957 Whitehall was occupied by the Pre-Federal Interim Government prior to the establishment of the West Indies Federation in 1958. In 1963, it became the Office of the Prime Minister occupied by The Hon. Dr. Eric Williams, Trinidad and Tobago's first Prime Minister after Independence.

Restored in 2000, Whitehall continued to be occupied by the Office of the Prime Minister of the Republic of Trinidad and Tobago until 2009.

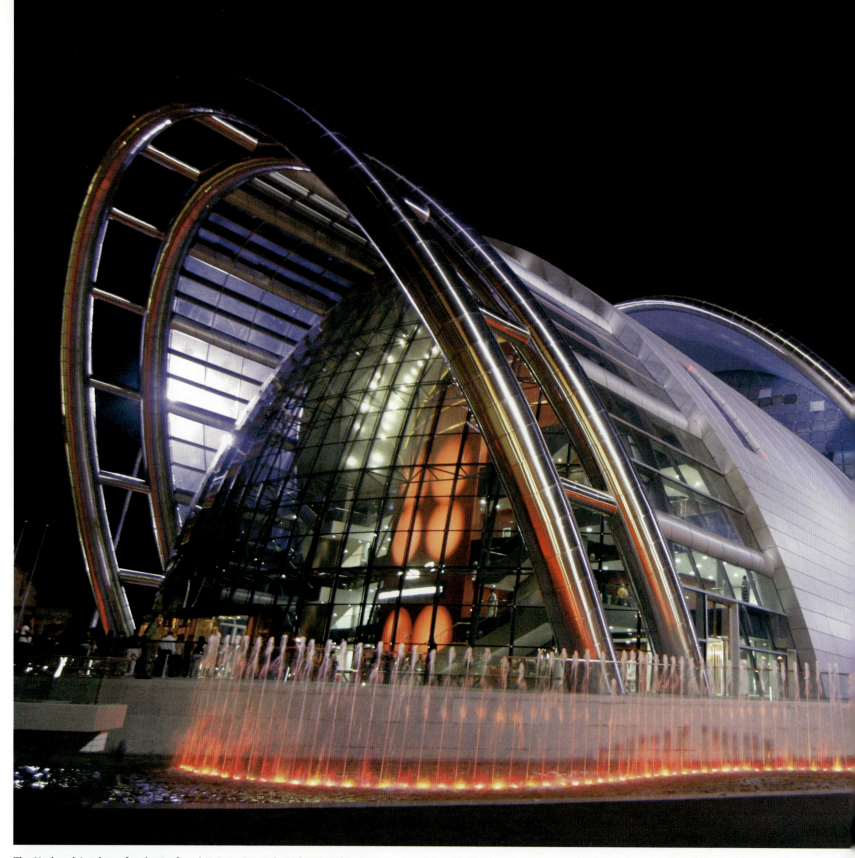

The National Academy for the Performing Arts, Queen's Park, Port of Spain

Interior of the National Academy for the Performing Arts

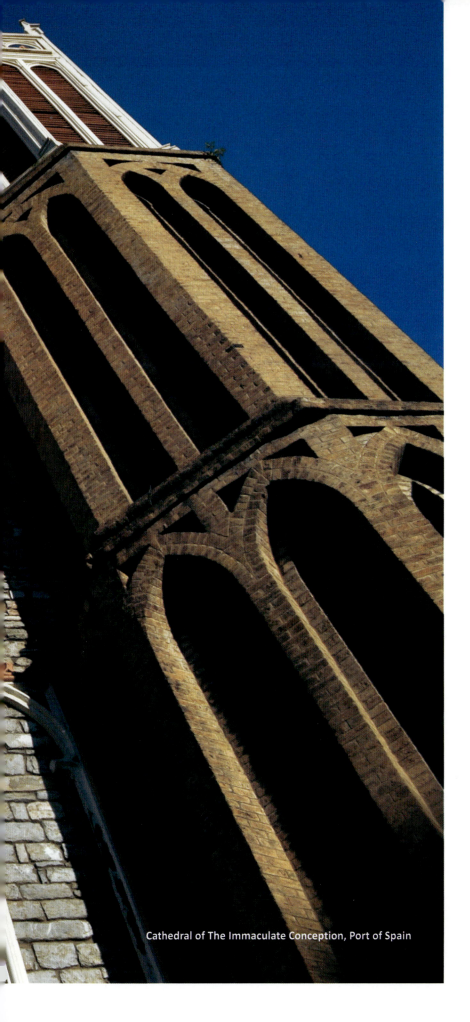
Cathedral of The Immaculate Conception, Port of Spain

Monumental Expressions
of Faith

Across the architectural landscape of Trinidad and Tobago there is an unmistakable visibility of a vast range of structures which were built and dedicated as houses of worship. There are cathedrals, mandirs, mosques, synagogues, temples and various types of churches. From the very modest to the very grandest, these edifices represent the remarkable number of religious groups contained within this comparatively small geographical land mass.

It is noteworthy, generally speaking, that many people are often identified by their religious affinity as much as they may be recognized by their nationality or ethnicity. Through the rich heritage of this southernmost Caribbean Island, ranging from the pre-columbian to the confluence of the colonists and the diverse diasporas, the legacies of ritualistic practices, religions and persuasions of faith have been significant cultural components which have substantively contributed to the formation of the national psyche.

Trinbagonians are proud practitioners of their faith. Numerous groups of pious devotees are widely distributed among a seemingly numberless array of religions including Anglicans, Hindus, Methodists, Muslims, Presbyterians, Roman Catholics, Seventh Day Adventists and Wesleyans. Added to these larger and varied denominations, there are the Afro-Caribbean faiths of the Shouter or Spiritual Baptists and the Orisha sects. One of the fastest growing groups among all worshippers is the Evangelical or Pentecostal movement. They are considered to be very charismatic and fundamentalist in their religious expression. Additional smaller groups include The Church of Jesus Christ of Latter-day Saints, Jehovah's Witness and certain other New Age factions.

Statue of Christ the Liberator at Mount St. Benedict. A creation of Pat Chu Foon in 1975

As with many nations, the strand of religion is closely woven into the cultural evolution and development of the people of Trinidad and Tobago. The multi-ethnic, multi-racial and pluralistic populace in this twin-island state is a descendant group of those migrants who were compelled to journey from their particular mother cultures across the oceans of fate. They carried their houses of worship with them, not as external bundles of wood and stone tied to their collective backs, but rather as treasured schematic plans carefully hidden in the cargo-holds of their hearts. Upon alighting and being liberated in their new found settings, they unfurled the blueprints of their transported heart's designs and recreated the structures of their origins. Thus, they erected religious monuments to enshrine their expressions of faith.

Designed by East Indian architects, the beautiful pink facade of the Ganapathi Sachchidananda Ashrama at Orangefield Road, Carapichaima

The colourful fresco ceiling of the St. Vincent Ferrer Roman Catholic Church in Grand Chemin, Moruga

Parishioner faithfully polishes a candle stand at St Margaret's Anglican Church in Belmont, Port of Spain

"Our Lady of Montserrat" RC Church is located in the hills of the Central Range in the village of Tortuga. This wooden church was built by its first priest Fr. Marie Jules Dupoux and opened in December 24, 1878. The church takes its name from the Montserrat Hills where it is situated. These hills got their name from the early Spanish settlers who likened them to the Montserrat Mountains in the heartland of the Catalunya region in Spain.

Temple By The Sea, Waterloo

The Temple in the Sea

This beautiful East Indian temple evokes a certain sense of rarity. At the serene village location of Waterloo on the West coast of Trinidad, in the Gulf of Paria, the *Temple in the Sea* stands demurely just off shore and connected to the mainland by a narrow isthmus for access. It's quaint appearance stirs fascination.

This picturesque edifice is a legacy of Siewdass Sadhu, an East Indian indentured labourer and a committed worshipper. With a deep personal conviction to have a special place of worship in the area, Sadhu set out to build a temple singlehandedly. In 1947 his first effort was erected on lands owned by the sugar cane company, Tate and Lyle. It was broken down and Sadhu was charged with trespassing and fined £100 or 14 days in prison for his infraction.

Undaunted by the experience, the purpose of the visionary prevailed. For twenty-five years, this determined devotee, with the use of his bicycle for transporting materials, persisted to the fulfilment of his dreams.

Now perched in the midst of the quiet ebb and flow of the Gulf of Paria waters, the *Temple in the Sea* portrays a testimonial of the strength of the human will in the pursuit of human endeavour.

The Jinnah Memorial Mosque (Exterior), St. Joseph

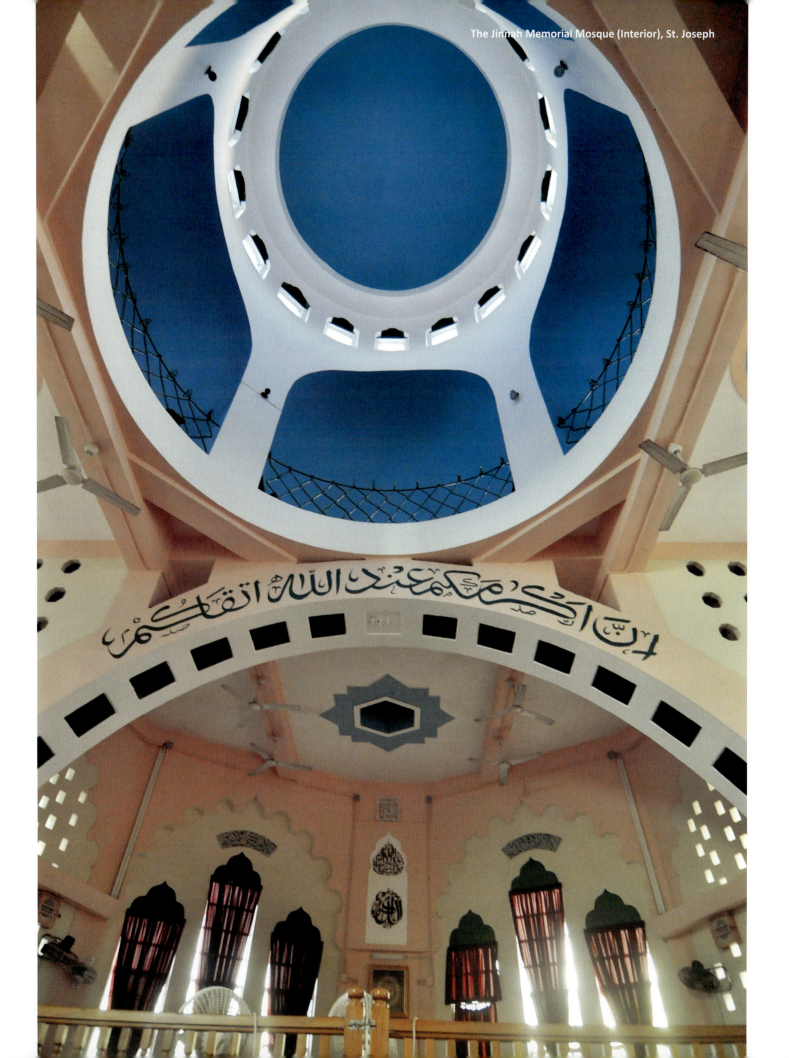
The Jinnah Memorial Mosque (Interior), St. Joseph

The 85 foot murti (statue) of Lord Hanuman, the Hindu God of strength located in Orangefield, Carapichaima

The Archbishop's House, Port of Spain

Hindu Temple, Debe

109

National Festivals & Observances

The soul of a nation is revealed through the social expressions of its people.

There are no grey areas in the social spectrum of the people of Trinidad and Tobago. Every form of life in the daily agenda here is awash with a kaleidoscope of colour, a rhapsody of sound and a swirl of activity. The pace is frenetic, the beat is throbbing, the rhythm is animated and the energy is unrelenting. Everyone and everything appear to be directed by some national choreographer in a theatrical ambience that is perpetually resounding with the tempo of tropical melodies.

It is no accident that *Trinbagonians* are readily given to elaborate expressions in art and music. Their creations are a national patch-quilt of diverse elements that form the identity of this land of mesmerizing colour. It perhaps can be likened to the varied notes on the *'tenor pan'* (steel pan) of the famed national musical instrument. Though each note is different and distinct, yet when played together skilfully by the *'panist'*, a collective sound like no other fills the air and captivates the attention with a commanding statement.

A *Trinbagonian* is unmistakable! He is a standard bearer of the soul of his nation. Typically, he is vividly and vocally expressive! From where does all this showiness emanate? The many cultures represented in the national landscape each have their own social expression and contribution. As the population evolves and blends together, united expressions reflect a celebration of boundless liberty from speckled histories of various forms of restraint.

Festivals in Trinidad and Tobago are as wide-ranging as its people. Life in Trinidad and Tobago is never dull. There are seemingly countless cultural festivals. Religious and ceremonial activities abound. The commemoration of national independence is notable. The arrival of the different races and the emancipation of people of African origins are recognized. *Trinbagonians* cherish their freedom and keenly enjoy occasions when they can *'free up'* - liberate their inner being, in celebrations of their choice.

> "No, no, don't stop the Carnival."

Year in and year out across the land of Trinidad and Tobago, there seems to be a native cycle of an unending happy atmosphere which appears to be saying, ***"No, no, don't stop the Carnival."***

Stick Fighting in Trinidad and Tobago

The crack and clatter of the sticks echo as they violently crash against each other. There are shouts of *"Bois, Bois!"* (French for "Wood, Wood!"). There is an incessant pulsating drumming which evokes a certain ancient rumbling sound. There is a swaying crowd shadowing the moves of the combatants. The setting is an arena called a *Gayelle*. This is *Kalinda* - stick-fighting in Trinidad and Tobago. It is a type of martial art developed by descendants of African slaves under the French colonists. It was also a ritual by which many males of a village asserted their manhood.

From around the 1860's, stick fighting in Trinidad and Tobago became a noted event in the pre-Carnival period. The *Kalinda* fighters took on a famed notoriety during the *Canboulay* Riots of 1881 in Port of Spain. They gathered themselves against the colonial British police to physically defend the right to celebrate the beloved Carnival of the masses.

From Tabaquite, Freeport, Moruga and villages across the nation, the *Boismen* gather in the centre of the *Gayelle*. The *Chantuelle* (Chantwell), who are the song-leaders, chorus their songs of encouragement and derision. The drum-beat throbs. There are bleeding knuckles and bleedings heads as the stick-fighters' sticks clash. Again the cries go up, *"Bois, Bois!"*

In the Gayelle - Stick fighting finals in Mayaro, South Trinidad.

Canboulay

The *Canboulay* commemorative festival is an integral part of the history of Carnival in Trinidad and Tobago. From deep within the fabric of the national cultural development, *Canboulay*, or properly termed, **"Cannes Brulées",** which means "burnt cane", became a notable celebration by the descendants of former slaves. The event largely came from the seasonal task of extinguishing cane fires so that the harvest of sugarcane would not be lost. *Canboulay* evolved into an important social expression by the black people of the period and became marked by great excitement, festivities and the carrying of lighted torches along the streets.

In the early 1880's, a significant dimension was added to the events of *Canboulay*. The local police authorities sought to bring an end to the *Canboulay* festivities citing public disorder and potential danger of towns being burnt down due to the lighted flambeaux carried by many of the revellers. Many riots and street fights broke out between ex-slave cane workers and the police. The seriousness of the conflicts resulted in loss of life. However, the *Canboulay* festivals would not be quenched and remained as a vibrant expression of a people determined to be no longer restrained.

Over the years, the *Canboulay* celebrations have emerged and continue to this present time as a noted prelude to Carnival in Trinidad and Tobago. Marked by lively social portrayals of times past, there is dancing and stick fighting with various scenes depicting the enslavement and struggles of former times.

Canboulay Riots portrayals - British authorities arrayed against ex-slave sugarcane workers

A gang of ex-slaves sugarcane workers armed with sticks ready for confrontation with their British antagonists

Carnival 'Trinbagonian' Style

The uninhibited expressions of the diverse masses... The flamboyant display of the most colourful and incredible costumes... The uniquely reverberating rhythmic sounds of *'soca'* and *'steelband'* music... The streets filled with thousands of dancing and prancing masqueraders... This is Carnival in Trinidad and Tobago at its most spectacular!

In Trinidad and Tobago, Carnival is unquestionably the most celebrated of all its national festivals. It is an enormous festive outpouring that emphatically demonstrates a happy character trait within the overall national psyche of *Trinbagonians.* It is the product of over two centuries of social, cultural and artistic evolution.

At the core of Carnival in Trinidad and Tobago, there is an underlying statement that commemorates, with an unfettered release of personal exuberance, what it means to be set free from all symbols of slavery. It spans and embraces the diversity of resident experiences and influences in generations of its people. Deep in the roots of this event are distinct traces of unbridled African tribal gaiety, the pomp of 18th century French pageantry and the varied cultural inputs, illustrative of the panoply of people who have made these islands their home.

The culture of Carnival is as varied as its people. Seemingly, no sooner the previous year's Carnival comes to an end on the Tuesday night preceding Ash Wednesday, anticipation and preparation for the next year begins. Immediately after Christmas the carnival season starts in earnest. The framework that carries this event is comprised of the traditional calypso singers, and their more contemporary colleagues known as *'soca'* artistes, launching their new songs for the season. The music centres on the many steel pan orchestras and brass bands fine-tuning their preferred melodies. Costume designers feverishly create their eye-catching regalia for their massive entourage of masqueraders. The melting-pot of Trinidad and Tobago Carnival by this time is near boiling-point.

The six remaining days of this festive jamboree begins with the re-enactment of the *'Canboulay Riots'* commemorating the conflicts between the freed slaves and the British police

during the 1880's. Later in the day, there is a series of splendid presentations of *'ole-time'* traditional masquerade which showcases many of the original characters of this colourful art-form. The Friday before Carnival is known as **'Fantastic Friday'** when the event really explodes into a frenzy and glitzy crescendo at the numerous parties and shows around the country. On Saturday during the day, the children have their 'Kiddies Carnival' parade where even the tiny-tots can be seen in their cute costumes jumping and skipping as the music fills the air. Later that night, the steel-pan competition will be concluded with the crowning of a new **Panorama** steel-orchestra champion for the best musical presentation on the national instrument. Sunday will be the no-holds-barred and flamboyant **Dimanche Gras**, the parading of the grandest of costume exhibits from which the king and queen of Carnival are judged. Also, the Calypso Monarch is crowned for the most popularly delivered musical and lyrical social commentary. Merriment across the nation reaches a pulsating high-point. On Monday at dawn, revelers from Sunday night parties and *'Ole Mas* characters parade along the streets in a range of J'Overt bands. The spectacle of *'Ole Mas* consists of characters in comical disguises and their performances which satirize people in high places or ridicule the foibles of society. After the unrestrained revelry of **J'Ouvert Morning**, the rest of Monday and into Tuesday, masquerade bands burst out in their colourful masses, some in their many thousands of members broken into dozens of processional sections. The nation's streets become the world's largest stage where gaiety in its most extravagant abandonment takes place – **This is Carnival *Trini* style!**

Traditional & Modern
Masquerade Characters

To the uninitiated, the spectacle of the thousands of masqueraders at Carnival in Trinidad and Tobago may appear to be just a jumble of colours, caricatures and costumes. On the contrary! There are many meaningful and meticulous processes which are perfected to the most fastidious detail to achieve the specifically desired Carnival expression.

All ages enjoy and participate in the gaiety and festivities of the season. From 'Kiddies Carnival' on Carnival Saturday to the huge parades on Carnival Tuesday, masqueraders take to the streets in all their splendor.

Present-day revelers choose from two forms of costumes —Traditional or Modern. This distinction is demonstrated from the pre-dawn masquerade macabre of **J'Ouvert Morning** on Carnival Monday, to the more colourful splendour of **Carnival Tuesday**. Masqueraders are very purposeful in the choice of their costume to best convey the portrayal of their fantasy.

Traditional masquerade characters include: *Baby Doll, Bats, Bookman, Burrokeet, Sumayree, Cow Band, Dame Lorraine, Fancy Indians, Jab-Jab, Jab Molassie, Midnight Robber, Minstrels, Moko Jumbie, Negue Jadin, Pierrot Grenade and Sailor Mas*. Many of these characters are a satirical parody on elements of African culture, slavery and early colonial times. Some depict characters in later history coming from the cinema and the two World Wars.

In today's modern masquerade the creation of many costumes has shifted from the traditional fabrics and designs to a more international appearance which mainly features bikinis, beads, and feathers. Hugely popular among the masses of the young and young at heart, this distinctively *Trinbagonian* accent on the 'Rio-Las Vegas Showgirl' genre exhibits a temperature of Carnival which may be described simply as, *"Hot, Hot, Hot!"*

Kiddies Carnival

Among the many activities during the Saturday of the Carnival weekend, children who take part in the festivities are brought to the streets and parade venues to make their mark on this very celebrated national event. Termed *'Kiddies Carnival'*, the children take on all the familiar masquerade characters as they perform in their various age-group competitions. With accompanying parents in tow, and the young masses dancing, jumping and strutting to the music, everyone is a winner as they file past the pageant judges.

With hundreds of schools and community organizations participating in *Kiddies Carnival*, children get an opportunity to develop stronger friendships, and learn more about their culture as *Trinbagonians* whilst they enjoy an experience they will always cherish.

Devil Masquerade

Of the many variations of 'devil masquerade' which became popular in the early history of Carnival in Trinidad and Tobago, those which took lasting prominence were the *imp, jab jab, jab molassie*, and the *devil*. Before emancipation, slaves were not allowed to participate in Carnival openly. However, at the end of slavery, their new found liberty allowed their now unbridled fervor a place in public festivities. Born out of the legacy of the harsh repression of slavery, slaves sought to dress themselves as fearsome 'beasts' and acted out hellish scenes characterizing the days of slavery. As a mark of reflective indignation on display, recently liberated slaves covered themselves in black grease, molasses, or some gooey substances taking to the streets to revel in their freedom. Their enjoyment was seemingly two-fold, personal merriment and the pleasure of offending and antagonizing the upper classes whom they sought to offend as a type of social recompense for decades of suffering.

Nowadays, the stage for the band of devil masqueraders opens on Carnival Monday morning. Referred to as *J'Ouvert*, festivities begin before sunrise at 4:00am. The grand release of the many variations on the 'devil mas' set off to roam the streets fervently gyrating to the cacophony of 'rhythm section' music. The range of devil themes including, the *Dirty Mas, Mud Mas and Blue Devils*. This traditional form of masquerade is collectively called *Jab Molassie*. All these 'devil' masqueraders depict a sense of revenge. Their threats are acts of retribution for crimes done to them in the past.

The term *'jab'* is derived from the French patois word 'diable', meaning devil. *'Molassie'* is the patois for the French word *Mélasse*, which is molasses. The famous *Jab Molassie* character represents the ghost of a slave who met his death by falling into a vat of boiling molasses in a sugar factory. The *Jab Molassie* characters would carry chains with locks and keys around their waists to create a make-believe scuffle and uproar in which others would tug at them as if to bring restraint conjuring a parody of pandemonium.

Rising out of the cloak of the pre-dawn darkness, these are some of the frenzied scenes that mark Carnival Monday morning across Trinidad and Tobago.

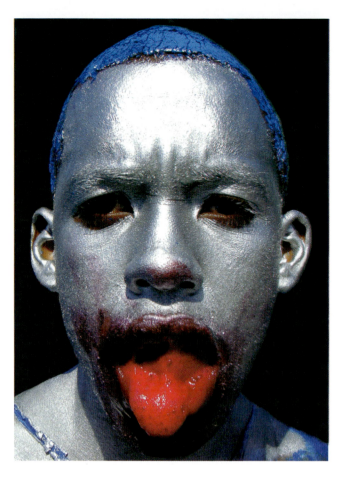

Midnight Robber

The very distinctive *Midnight Robber* remains one of the most beloved characters in the traditional masquerade of carnival.

This masquerader is immediately recognized by his mainly black costume - satin shirt and pantaloons, looking like a Mexican cowboy in the American wild-west tradition. He also wears a black, flowing cape, on which the skull and cross bones are painted. A huge black-fringed and broad-brimmed hat completes his attire. He often carries a weapon - a dagger, sword or gun. He may be seen with a wooden money box in the shape of a coffin. He carries a whistle which he blows to punctuate his tales of valour.

He can sometimes be heard shouting his famed "Robber Talk" - extravagant boastful brags of his supposed exploits, strength, and invincibility. This "Robber Talk" is derived from the tradition of the African *'Griot'* or storyteller; he is also declares or proclaims a satire of his former slave master. "Robber Talk" has become a carry-over from Carnival into the local folk idiom. Whenever people boast about their prowess in physical skills, they are mockingly accused of engaging in "Robber Talk", if their listeners do not think they are capable of doing what they threaten.

Moko Jumbie

Towering high above everyone at Carnival is the unmistakable masquerade called the *Moko Jumbie*. This popular traditional character is an authentic African masquerader that walks on stilts which can be as tall as 12 feet. His costume would typically be long brightly coloured suit and pants or gown draping down over his stilts.

'Moko' is a West African god which in the Congo language also conveys a type of spiritualist or seer. In the same manner, the term 'jumbie' refers to a type of ghost. Together, a Moko Jumbie is to have the ability to foresee evil spirits faster than ordinary men because of his great height. The Moko Jumbie was therefore seen as a guard to the local village.

Jab Jab

Like jab molassie, the jab jab is one of the many incarnations of the devil masquerade in Carnival.

The jab jab has a similar name to the jab molassie, but has followed a different historical development path. The jab jab's costume makes him look like a medieval European jester. He is typically arrayed in two-coloured satin shirts with points at the waist. Additionally, his attire would be adorned with bells, mirrors, and rhinestones. He may have a flowing cape with a hood. He would also wear fancy stockings on his legs. The jab jab's getup may appear clownish, but it is intended to disguise the fierce warrior who carries a thick whip, ready to use in battle against any other jab jab he may encounter. The jab jab shows off his readiness for action with furious and intimidating chants rebelling against civil society.

Jab jab is called "the pretty devil" because it is unlike the black-faced bare-skinned jab molassie, or blue devil characters usually seen on Carnival Monday J'Ouvert morning. One of the distinguishing marks of the jab jab is his whip. It is said that he may carry two types of whips, one for fighting and the other for cracking. The second whip is whirled through the air and briskly snapped to create a frightfully exploding sound intended to strike fear in all those who are standing close by – another one of the unique sounds of Carnival in Trinidad and Tobago.

Fancy Indians

The Fancy Indian masquerade has remained ever popular among masqueraders. Various types of American Indians are portrayed ranging from North American tribal Indians to the Warahoons of the South American Orinoco delta region. These Indians are often termed as Red Indians, Black Indians, Blue Indians and many variants in between.

The primary feature of the Fancy Indian's costume is often the headpiece. It is worn with feathers sticking upward, and more feathers trailing down the back of the masquerader. Bright and colourful, the artisan's creation is elaborate and very meticulous. In some cases, much research done by band-leaders and mas-designers has led to presentations of costumes that closely resemble these worn by Native American Indians. The materials used include ostrich plumes, mirrors, beads, feathers, papier-mâché, and ribbons. Fully decked out in their spray of colours, Fancy Indian bands can comprise a warrior chief and his family, a group of chiefs, or a group of warriors.

Interestingly, these masqueraders dramatise Indian war dances and chant different versions of what seem to be war-cries. However, the authenticity of this language handed down from Indian masquerade veterans (the masquerade masters) has not been established!

Fancy Sailor

Traditional Masquerade Characters

Dame Lorraine

Cow Mas

Burrokeet Mas

Bat Mas

Minstrels

Phagwah

The East Indian spring festival of *Phagwa* or *Holi* has been celebrated in Trinidad since the first East Indian labourers arrived on these shores in 1845. At the end of the winter season, people gather in villages and temples to perform and sing festive *chowtal* songs to rejoice at the arrival of spring. The main day, *Holi*, also known as *Dhuli Vandana* in Sanskrit, also *Dhulheti Dhulandi* or *Dhulendi*, is celebrated with great happiness and animation by people throwing coloured powder and coloured water at each other. Great bonfires are lit the day before, which is also known as *Holika Dahan* (burning of *Holika*).

These often large bonfires are lit to commemorate, according to legend, *Prahlad's* victory over fire when his father, the demon-king *Hiranyakashipu* , wanted to punish him because he was a faithful devotee of the god *Vishnu*. The wicked king prompted his sister *Holika* to carry the lad into the fire making her believe that she would withstand the fire but the boy would be burnt. However, as *Holika* entered the fire, she was burnt, but *Prahlad* miraculously escaped without any injury because of his steadfast devotion to Vishnu.

So the grand *Phagwa* festivities also commemorate the victory of good over evil. These events are extremely happy occasions which are enjoyed by all who join in. The celebrations include bands of *tassa* drummers and singers with everyone washed in purple coloured water, *abeer*, and dyed in coloured powder.

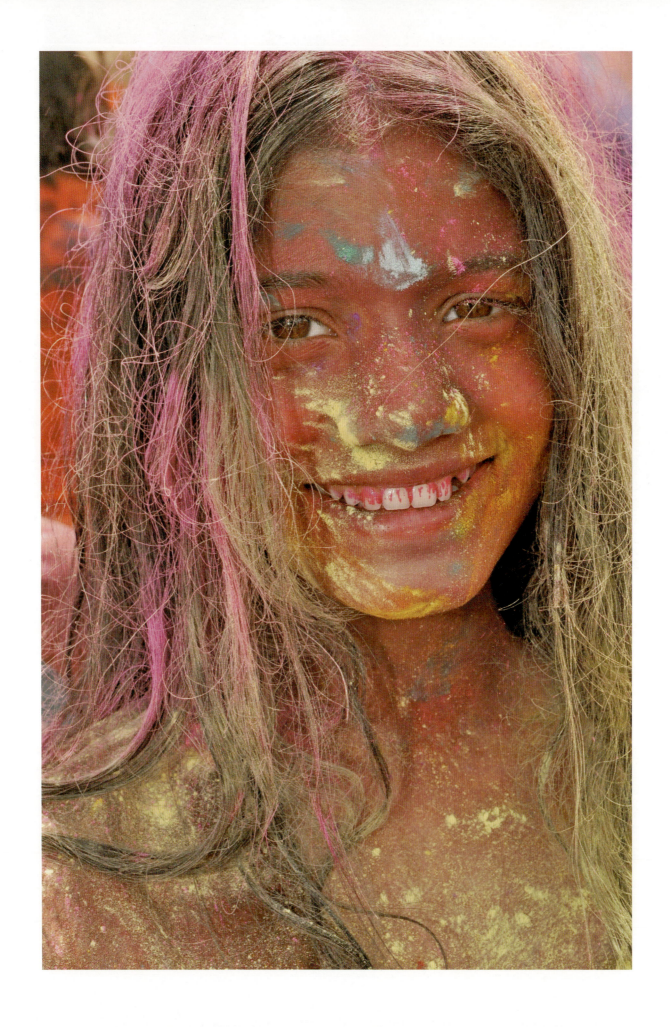

Spiritual Shouter Baptist Liberation Day

The Spiritual Shouter Baptists of Trinidad and Tobago celebrate their freedom of worship on the 30th of March each year. This date marks the abolition of the order which forbade participation in this African-influenced religion.

From 1917 to 1951 the Spiritual and Shouter Baptist faith was banned in Trinidad and Tobago by the colonial government of the day. The legislation to enact this ban was called the Shouters Prohibition Ordinance and it was passed on the 16th of November 1917. The reason given for the ordinance was that the Shouters made too much noise with their loud singing, frenzied shaking and bell ringing which was deemed a disturbance to the peace.

After much lobbying, the bill to repeal the ordinance was passed on the 30th of March 1951. The Spiritual and Shouter Baptists were now free to practice their religion. In 1996 this religious body gained further entitlement in their fight for recognition as the then ruling United National Congress government granted them an annual national public holiday.

The Spiritual and Shouter Baptist faith is an Afro-Caribbean religion which combines elements of traditional West African religions with Christianity. The Baptist faith was brought to Trinidad by the so called *"Merikins"*, former American slaves who were recruited by the British to fight for them during the wars against America from 1812 to 1814. After the end of these wars, the ex-slaves were settled as free men in south Trinidad in locations called Company villages in the Moruga area.

With their indigenous form of spiritual identity preserved, every 30th of March has become the date when this community of worshippers fervently celebrates Baptist Liberation Day. The event commemorates the repeal of the Shouters Prohibition Ordinance of 1917 granting the legal right and freedom of religious expression.

Christian Celebrations of Easter

For many *Trinbagonians* passion in religion can be as fervent as with any other social activity. During the Easter season, Christians in Trinidad and Tobago take part in a series of church services to commemorate the death, burial and resurrection of Jesus Christ. It is one of the most important occasions in the Christian calendar.

Across the wide variety of denominations, Easter celebrations reach their peak during Holy Week. This revered seven-day period starts on Palm Sunday, one week before Easter Sunday. During these days there are various re-enactments of the events some refer to as the 'Passion of Christ'. Palm Sunday is held in remembrance of the coming of Jesus to Jerusalem, where people waved palms and laid them on the ground along his path. Christian churches in Trinidad and Tobago join with the worldwide Christian fraternity to observe this event by the distribution of palm leaves to followers during their Palm Sunday services.

On the Friday of Holy week called Good Friday, this is the day observed as the day when Christ was crucified. Some churches including Roman Catholics perform a procession that symbolizes the retracing of the steps of Christ on his journey to crucifixion. This is called the Stations of the Cross. The Easter week is concluded with a high note of celebrations. Easter Sunday is also referred to as Resurrection Sunday. This is the day when Christ was resurrected form the dead in all His glory. For all Christians, it is the time of their greatest celebrations.

Catholic Priest rides a donkey at Palm Sunday procession in Talparo, Central Trinidad.

La Divina Pastora
& Soparee Mai

At every Easter in the town of Siparia in South Trinidad there is a special gathering of the united faithful. Roman Catholic and Hindu devotees form an alliance of worship as they converge at the La Divina Pastora RC Church to pay homage to a very special statue which is held in equal esteem by both groups.

To the Roman Catholics, the statue is known as La Divina Pastora, the Divine Shepherdess - the Blessed Virgin Mary. To the Hindus, the same figurine is revered as Soparee Mai, the Mother of Siparia, representing the Goddess Kali. For both sets of believers the artefact represents a special channel of hope for special blessings and healings.

Historically, Siparia was said to be a traditional of the Orinoco Indians. As a mark of recognition to this ancient vestige, a group of Spanish Capuchin Priests from Venezuela, and originally from the Santa Maria province of Aragon in Spain, sought to build a mission there. Specific dates *when devotion to La Divina Pastora was introduced to Trinidad are not known. However, records from the parish indicate that the statue was brought from Venezuela to Siparia by the Spanish priests in 1871.*

For Catholics, the Easter festivity is a preamble to the actual Feast of La Divina Pastora which is celebrated on May 15. This is when the statue is carried through the streets of Siparia and returned to the church which bears its name. In a great atmosphere of celebration and worship the Marian hymns are sung along with recitations of the rosary.

Hindus began paying homage to the Saint in deference to a famous legend. There are accounts which report that a young girl had been seen wandering in the pasture on which the church was to be later built. East Indian labourers at the time told villagers that by night fall, the same young girl had miraculously grown into an old woman. Hindus also revere the site as a place where many bring their young boys to be given their first haircut by special barbers. It is believed that when the boys have their hair cut on Good Friday here they will grow into strong, healthy men.

For over a hundred years, sectors of the Trinbagonian faithful extol their devotions to their beloved figure side by side. There are people bearing gifts for the saint, and others seeking alms. *The expectations of both are common. There is the single pursuit of a miracle.*

Mud volcano puja in Cedros, Southwest Trinidad.

Mud Volcano Pujas

Near the tip of the south western peninsula, at the town of Cedros, one of the twenty known mud volcanoes of Trinidad can be found. As one of the larger and more active volcano sites, this feature found at the Columbia coconut estate in the Fullerton area is held in sacred regard. Every year there are ceremonial rituals performed around the volcano by Hindu worshippers. The local residents often hear the gurgling and bubbling sound of the mud emanating from the location. To the predominant Hindu villagers, the sound challenges them to perform *pujas* (prayers) near the volcano. They believe that their offerings will pacify *Mother Durga,* the god of the land, causing her not to be angry with them and cause a great eruption from the mud volcanoes in the area.

Mud volcanoes are also called 'sedimentary volcanoes', they do bear a close relationship with the more familiar magmatic volcanoes. Mud volcanoes can erupt similar to magmatic volcanoes. They can spew out masses of hydrocarbon gases and tons of mud. Mud volcanoes have a direct relationship to oil and gas fields. They are direct indicators of the existence of hydrocarbons in the vicinity. They are essentially channels for releasing pressurized gas and mineral water, sometimes with traces of oil, together with associated mud from great depths. The mud volcano is active with constant emissions of bubbling hot water and soft clay. Fine sediments flow through surface cracks which form cones as they cool. Typically, the formation of these cones rises to no more than three feet.

Kali (Hindu deity) devotees carry kargam pots decorated with attractive flower arrangements into the sea.

Ganga Dhara

The festival of Ganga Dhara is a Hindu pilgrimage during which devotees offer their acts of worship to the mother of the ocean, Ganga, and the earth, Dharti.

This religious procession is known as a *Teerath*. It is recognized as a significant element within the Hindu religion. It speaks of a place of special spiritual connection and relation which people have with the land and sea.

For its devotees, the festival is seen as a way to preserve an ancient Hindu tradition. The event is to be celebrated in a pristine, serene setting where participants can focus on their relationships with Deity, the earth and themselves.

A dip in the ocean, where the Ganga drains into the sea is considered to be of great religious significance. A primary location where Ganga Dhara is celebrated in Trinidad is on the Marrianne River at the north coast town of Blanchisseuse. It features a wonderfully colourful event echoing its origins on the Ganges River in India. The day's event begins with dedicated women preparing a *puja,* prayer offering, for Lord Ganesh on a table set in the middle of the riverbed. To accommodate the worshippers, tents, platforms and ramps are set in place. With everything ready, there are processions along the riverbed with singing and offerings presented throughout the course of the day.

For the Hindu faithful, Ganga Dhara is a pilgrimage of worship and an occasion during which opportunities for particular blessings of desire are available. The date and time when Ganga Dhara is celebrated is determined by the lunar calendar.

Hindu devotees float yellow buttercups along the Marianne River in Blanchisseuse as an offering to Mother Ganga.

Yellow buttercups are gathered in this sari as offerings to be floated down the Marianne River at Blanchisseuse on the North coast.

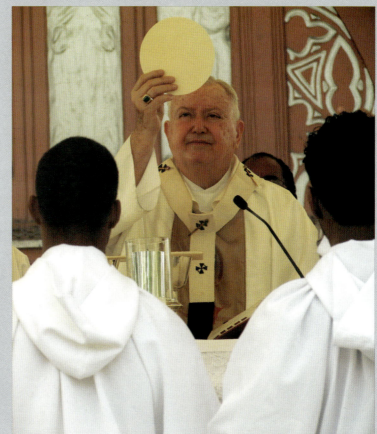

Corpus Christi Processions

Corpus Christi is one of the oldest holidays observed in Trinidad and Tobago. It is a religious feast introduced into Trinidad during the Spanish colonial period 1498-1797, and is celebrated by Roman Catholics worldwide. Roman Catholics believe that the bread and wine consecrated by a priest during Mass truly become the body and blood of Christ. The procession on the day of Corpus Christi, the Latin for Body of Christ, was introduced into Europe by the nun, St. Juliana of Liege in Belgium in AD1230. The purpose of the procession is to publicly venerate Christ's presence in the world. In Trinidad and Tobago, the procession normally starts at the Cathedral of the Immaculate Conception progressing westwards along the main thoroughfare, and returning to the Cathedral in the city of Port of Spain.

Under the terms of the Capitulation of 1797 when Trinidad was conquered by the British, Catholics were to be allowed to practice their faith as much as they wanted. This would have included the observance of Corpus Christi which is regarded as the quintessential Roman Catholic feast and national holiday. The procession is usually led by the Archbishop and a large representation of Catholic priests and lay persons. In the early British colonial period till 1840, the British Governors, though Anglican, and the military, participated in the grand event.

Priest blesses the boats off the waters of the fishing village Carenage for St. Peters day.

St. Peter's Day Celebrations

The St. Peter's Day celebrations hold a special place for many fisher-folk in Trinidad and Tobago. As an island, commercial fishing remains an important livelihood among the many fishing villages found along the nation's coastline. With many of these communities having a particular dependence on the fishing industry, there are time-honoured traditions which have been observed by generations of fisher-folk. This workforce's workplace is in the midst of the changeable elements of the high seas. A certain quality of hardiness and virtue is required to face the daily challenges of navigating the course to the next catch.

For many fisher-folk the occasion of the St. Peter's Day celebrations is an opportunity to pay homage to their patron saint, St. Peter, that principal Apostle among the twelve Disciples of Jesus Christ. St. Peter who was a fisherman by profession is regarded as fisher-folks' champion of the sea, fish and the skill of fishing. Admired as 'one of them', St. Peter is revered as a figure of comfort when faced with the waves of uncertainties as they cast their nets out in the ocean's depths.

Typically observed on June 29, or the last Sunday of June each year, those who recognise the tradition, participate in church services during the day and follow with the merriment of eating, drinking, and partying into the night. As a key aspect of the St. Peter's Day celebrations, some fisher-folk are accompanied by a priest or member of the clergy out unto the seas to receive pronouncements of blessings upon their lives, boats, nets, equipment and the waters where they ply their trade.

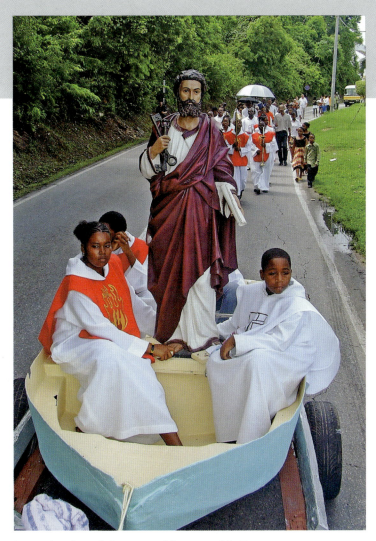

Procession through Carenage with statue of St. Peter, patron saint of fishermen.

Emancipation Day

Marking the anniversary of the abolition of slavery in 1834 to 1838, the national holiday called Emancipation Day is celebrated on the 1st of August each year with church services and festive street processions in Trinidad and Tobago.

The Emancipation Act presented by Thomas Buxton to the Parliament of the United Kingdom in 1833 to abolish slavery throughout most of the British Empire came into effect on the 1st of August 1834. Though the bill was enacted on that day however, absolute freedom was not immediate. Ex-slave masters were given the right to hold their former slaves to an apprenticeship period of a further four years beyond slavery until full release to total freedom. On August 1st, 1985, Trinidad and Tobago became the first country in the world to declare a national holiday to commemorate the abolition of slavery.

Eid-ul-Fitr

Eid-ul-Fitr is one of the most important festivals celebrated by Muslims. It is a time of deep dual emotions - sadness and jubilation. It is considered sad because the blessed month of *Ramadan* has ended. It is also seen as a time of great happiness because the month-long period of fasting has been completed.

Eid-ul-fitr is celebrated on the first day of *Shawwal*, the tenth month of the Islamic calendar. The sighting of the new crescent moon of that month marks the beginning of the event.

The term, *Eid-Ul-Fitr*, means to celebrate the breaking of the month of fasting. The beginning of the day of *Eid*, after dressing and having breakfast, people proceed to the mosques for the *Eid* prayer ceremony and recite the famous *Takbirat*, *"allahu akbar, allahu akbar,"* which means, Allah is the greatest. Muslims do not only celebrate the end of fasting, but they also thank God for the help and strength that has sustained them throughout the previous months. They also pray for help to practice self-control in their daily lives.

Amerindian Heritage Day

An ancient pre-dawn smoke signal ceremony typically marks the beginning of the annual Amerindian Heritage day celebrations. From the Arima location of the statue of the famed *Kalinago* warrior, *Hyarima*, descendants of Trinidad and Tobago's first nation people gather to launch each year's festivities.

Amerindian Heritage Day is commemorated to remind the remnant indigenous population about their place in the society of this twin-Island state as the lineage of the nation's first people.

During these times of cheer for this special group of *Trinbagonians*, there are wonderful presentations of indigenous craft, cuisine, and traditional clothing. Contributing to the multicultural charm of *Trinbagonian* music and dance, there is Amerindian drum-beating, cultural dance, singing, chanting and the playing of traditional wooden musical instruments.

For Amerindian Heritage Day, the Santa Rosa region of the city of Arima becomes the epicentre of the Carib community, reiterating the hallowed mark of the great Amerindian people of Trinidad and Tobago.

Carib Chief, Ricardo Bharath, makes an offering to the Amerindian ancestors

Orisha Worship

Among the many religions observed in Trinidad and Tobago, the practice of the Orisha faith is recognized as an undeniable component of the socio-religious framework of the nation's belief system.

Adherents of Orisha worship are largely of African descent. This religious tradition has its origins in the West African region and is widely practiced among the Yoruba people of Nigeria and neighboring states. As one of the great continent's oldest religions, its devotees heavily rely upon its varied observances to inform and guide their daily lives.

The Orisha religion in Trinidad and Tobago, like the other African-derived religions of the Americas and the Caribbean, came into existence when European colonialists brought millions of Africans to work on the thriving sugar, cotton, and tobacco plantations. The slaves to the so-called New World could bring no more than their physical bodies along with their customs and beliefs – legacy resources which have withstood the rigorous passage of time. Significant numbers of these forced workers were of the Yoruba people. As they were assimilated into the varying European sub-cultures in the new colonies, the Orisha practice took on differing names in different settings. In Cuba, Puerto Rico and the Dominican Republic, for example, this belief system is known as *Santeria*. In Brazil where there is widespread practice, it is known as *Candomble*. In Trinidad and Tobago, Orisha worship is often referred to as *Shango*.

Orisha observers in Trinidad and Tobago engage in a rich and complex set of rituals and methods of worship which are distinct to their order. Orishas are thought of as guardian spirits. The *Lucumi* Yoruba believe in one Higher Power. They call him *Olodumare*. They believe that each person has a Guardian Spirit called an *Orisha*. Orishas are representations of the Supreme Being that are manifested as forces of nature. For example, *Shango* is the Orisha of thunder. He is a warrior king; he is saluted by the term *"Cabio sile Shango"* when thunder is heard.

For Orisha practitioners in Trinidad and Tobago, their form of worship is held with great passion and pride. Theirs is a rich full-bodied ceremony which typifies an undiluted religious legacy from the equatorial depths of Africa.

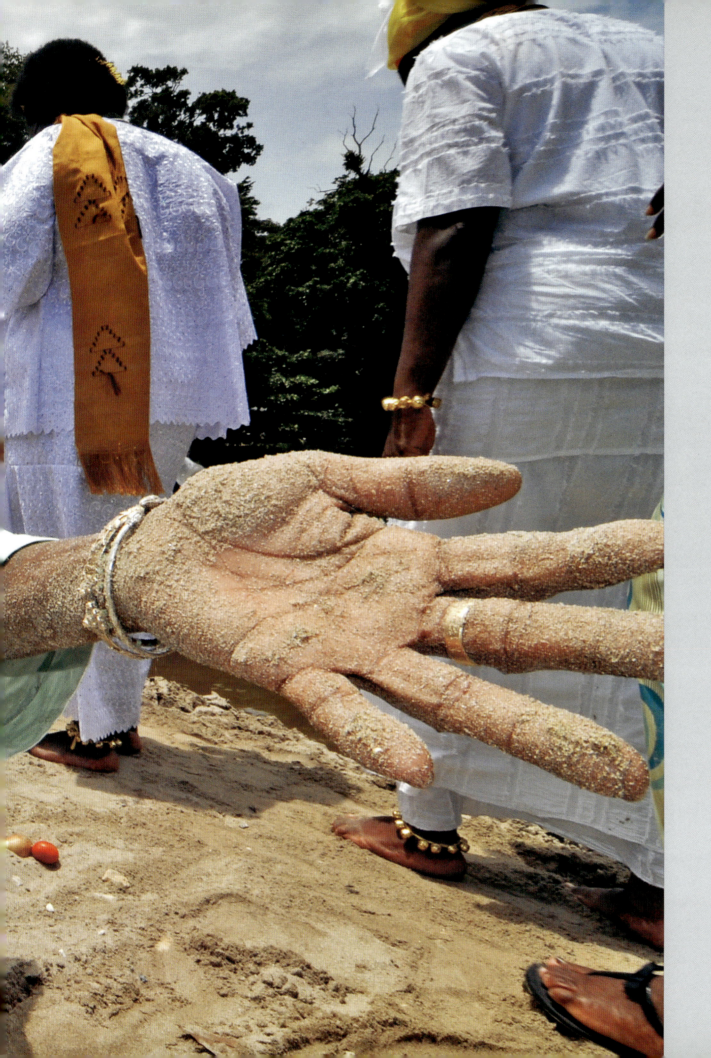

Ramleela

One of the great East Indian spiritual epics is the *Ramayan* legend of *Lord Rama's* heroic rescue of his abducted wife, *Sita*, from her kidnap by the demon called *Ravan,* the King of Lanka. The saga centres on *Rama* with the help of his brother, *Lakshma*n, and his most devoted servant *Lord Hanuman,* setting off on their journey for the eventual rescue of *Sita.*

Lord Rama is said to be the 7th incarnation of *Vishnu*, the Preserver. The *Ramayan* story is illustrative of the deep heart and character of India. It speaks of the virtues of devotion, loyalty, family roles and respect for elders. It is the pursuit of the victory of good over evil. The *Ramayan* account can be seen as a guide to living as ideal human beings.

The story concludes with *Lord Rama* reaping the benefits of remaining faithful to his life's purpose in the midst of great personal adversity. His reward was that he gained victory over *Ravan*, freed his wife and was eventually crowned as King of the province *Ayodhya*.

The figure of Ravan

Dance of the archers.

The figure of Lord Hanuman

The culmination of Ramleela is marked by the burning of an effigy of Ravan.

Divali celebrations in Felicity

Divali - Festival of Lights

One of the great East Indian spiritual epics is the *Ramayan* legend of *Lord Rama's* heroic rescue of his abducted wife, *Sita*, from her kidnap by the demon called *Ravan,* the King of Lanka. The saga centres on *Rama* with the help of his brother, *Lakshma*n, and his most devoted servant *Lord Hanuman,* setting off on their journey for the eventual rescue of *Sita.*

Lord Rama is said to be the 7th incarnation of *Vishnu*, the Preserver. The *Ramayan* story is illustrative of the deep heart and character of India. It speaks of the virtues of devotion, loyalty, family roles and respect for elders. It is the pursuit of the victory of good over evil. The *Ramayan* account can be seen as a guide to living as ideal human beings.

The story concludes with *Lord Rama* reaping the benefits of remaining faithful to his life's purpose in the midst of great personal adversity. His reward was that he gained victory over *Ravan*, freed his wife and was eventually crowned as King of the province *Ayodhya*.

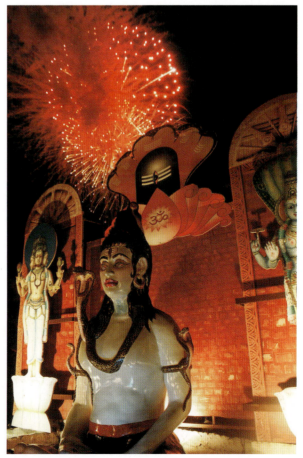

Fireworks at the Divali Nagar site.

Kartik Snaan

The festival of Kartik Snaan or Kartik Nahan usually follows soon after the more renowned Divali celebrations. It is observed in the same lunar month as Divali, the festival of lights. It is also the final major religious ceremony for Hindus in the calendar year.

Celebrated by thousands of Hindus throughout Trinidad and Tobago, the rituals of the celebration are usually observed by followers who go to the many rivers, or to the sea, to do *pujas* (prayers) and take spiritual baths called *snaan*. It is the general belief that sins or bad karmas are washed away or forgiven when these ceremonies are carried out.

For Hindus, all waterways become holy on the day that Kartik is observed, once they have been blessed during *pujas*. The most popular locations where Kartik is celebrated include Manzanilla Beach in the east, and Mayaro, Mosquito Creek and Cedros in the south of the island.

Kartik celebrations at Manzanilla on the East coast.

Tadjahs in St. Clair, Port of Spain.

Hosay

The festival Hosay is observed annually with colourful street parades commemorating the martyrdom in the year 680 AD of Hussain *(Hussein)*, the grandson of Muhammad, the Prophet of Islam.

After the death of the Prophet Muhammad in 632 AD, two Muslim factions of beliefs began concerning the selection of a successor *(caliph)*, Shiites or Shi'ah, and Sunnis. A great conflict arose between these two groups, the height of which brought about the slaying of Hussain, a Shiite, by Sunnis.

Shiites around the world observe Hosay in different ways. In Lucknow, India, the centre of Shiite culture in India, it is observed with great passion with tadjahs *(taziyas)*, drums, and mourners who re-enact the Battle of Kerbala with chants of *"Hussain!"* This custom was brought to Trinidad by East Indian Shiites who migrated from India in the 19th century. The first observance of Hosay in Trinidad has been traced back to 1854, eleven years after the first indentured labourers arrived from India. However, maintaining the Hosay tradition was not always an easy task. After a ban on all types of parades was imposed by the British colonialist government in 1884 following riots on sugar estates, approximately 30,000 people defiantly took to the streets to commemorate Hosay at Cipero Street, Toll Gate, Point-a-Pierre Road and Mon Repos in San Fernando, on Thursday, October 30th. According to eyewitness accounts handed down through the oral tradition, after the riot act was read, the Muslim devotees continued their procession shouting, *"Hosay, Hosay! Hosay, Hosay!"* British Police Chief, Captain Arthur Baker, ordered policemen to fire shots to disperse the crowd. During the course of events, 22 men were killed and another 120 were wounded. That fateful day is commonly referred to in Trinidad history as the Hosay or *Jahaaji* Massacre.

The martyrdom of Hussain is observed by all Shiites during Muharram, the first month of the Islamic lunar calendar. Due to the fact that the lunar year is about 11 days shorter than the Gregorian solar year, the observance takes place at different calendar-months each year.

The largest Hosay parades take place in two Shiite communities in Trinidad: St. James, in the western section of Port-of-Spain, in the north, and Cedros, on the southwest peninsula in the south. The St. James event is the largest. It draws thousands of spectators of all religions every year. The Shiites of St. James spend a considerable amount of time and money in the building of miniature temples with bamboo, wood, paper, and tinsel to depict the tomb of Hussain. The colourful spectacle of the drums and flags is a symbolic expression of what occurred during the wars in the 7th century.

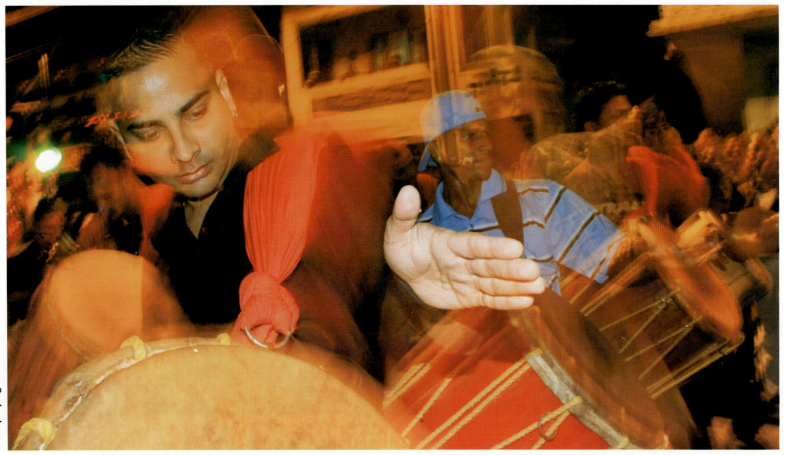

Tassa playing in St. James.

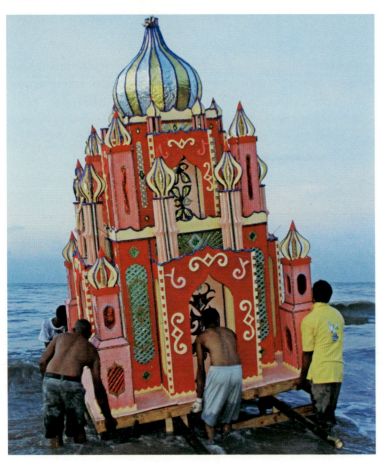

Moon dance.

Chinese Festivals in Trinidad and Tobago

Chinese festivals in Trinidad and Tobago feature a colourful array of activities which include the dragon dance, ribbon dance, lantern festival, lion dance and dragon boat racing. These are all Chinese commemorative events having centuries of traditions which are unique contributions to the range of all the local festivities in Trinidad and Tobago. Similar to other ethnic groups, Chinese descendants are equally far removed from their country of cultural origin, but as *Trinbagonian* nationals, they too occupy the cultural stage of this multi-community society with their distinct blend of amazing presentations.

Annual events which showcase these wonderful Chinese galas include the famed Chinese New Year's celebrations, China's national day and the dragon boat festival, all of which contribute towards commemorating the occasion of the first arrival of Chinese to Trinidad and Tobago in 1806. During these celebrations there are exhibitions of colourful costumes featuring the gaiety of dances to choreographies of ancient movements and the musical accompaniment of thunderous drum-beats. The displays can proceed throughout the day and evenings, then culminating with another gift to the world from the Chinese - fireworks at night.

House brightly lit with Christmas lights in Valsayn.

Parang singing reflects the rich Spanish/Venezuelan influence in Trinidad.

Christmas in Trinidad and Tobago

Family, friends and festivities are among the primary ingredients in a *Trinbagonian* Christmas. Beside all other festivals, for Christians and non-Christians alike, the Christmas season strikes a very merry chord for the people of the entire nation, in one form or other.

There is an unmistakable air of light-heartedness among the people. The senses are festively aroused by the distinct Christmas aromas which fill the atmosphere. The sound of *parang* music; the smell of cooked ham and black cake; the taste of sorrel, ginger beer and *ponche crème;* the sight of colourful lights and fancy decorations; and the feel of that special seasonal warmth and radiance in every soulful sentiment…

This is Christmas in Trinidad and Tobago!

Avocat Falls, Blanchisseuse

Eco-Systems
& Natural Wonders

The natural beauty of a nation is displayed in its geography, flora and fauna.

Reflections of the Caribbean typically evoke colourful images of tropical life found in idyllic settings. Representing the region's famed luxuriant landscape, the twin islands of Trinidad and Tobago not only boast a remarkable diversity of people and culture, but also an ecological paradise of geography, flora and fauna that is singular and stunning.

Featuring a combined landmass of some 5,128 km^2, the physical geography of these islands reveals that they were once connected to the South American mainland. One look at Trinidad's towering Northern Range of mountains displays a close likeness in their formation to the eastern extension of the great continental Andean chain. However, over many thousands of years, what may have been a terrain of adjoining plains and valleys became flooded by the rising oceans to form the expanse of sea between Trinidad and Venezuela now called the Gulf of Paria.

In looking at the plant and animal life of Trinidad and Tobago, one sees certain similarities to life on the mainland. However, the islands' flora and fauna habitation have followed their own way forward and determined a distinct course in their own natural evolution. Here, you will find a unique creation of an ecological community of bio diversity that ranges from the inconspicuous to the extravagant in true *Trinbagonian* style!

Trinidad and Tobago features a vast cross-section of vegetation that is verdant and vibrant. You will find trees ranging from evergreens to the leaf shedding variety – *purpleheart* to *blackheart*, the *mora* to the *bois-multre*. There are thousands of flowering plants, orchids, ferns, lilies and exotic plants in a cornucopia of colour extending beyond the imagination. Among them are the glowing orange blossoms of the *immortelle* and the alluring pink and yellow flowering *poui*.

There are more species of birds in Trinidad and Tobago than in any other Caribbean island. A trek along any hiking path can give a performance of dazzling sight and melodic sound from such birds as the *purple honeycreepers, tufted coquettes, blue-and-yellow macaws and the piping-guan,* locally called the *pawi*, a bird unique to Trinidad. Fluttering upon the gentle tropical breezes, there are butterflies from 620 species weaving a maze of colour through the air. There are numerous mammals which include the *agouti, anteater, armadillo, capuchin monkey, deer, howler monkey, tree porcupine, manatee, opossum* and *ocelot*. Reptiles feature *anacondas, caimans, iguanas, leatherback turtles* and *frogs* (the famed *golden tree frog* is also found here). Insects abound. There are all manner of crawling, flying, hopping insects – from the tiniest mite to the giant *white-witch moth*, a species said to have the largest wingspan of its kind known anywhere on earth!

From creatures to cultures, a spectacular integration of life!

Aside from the coastal waters of Trinidad and Tobago, which are particularly influenced by the great South American rivers of the Orinoco and the Amazon, there are two main swamps which discharge into the sea, the Caroni to the west and Nariva to the east of the island. These swamps contain intricate networks of mangroves and waterways, both fresh and salt. A whole world of bio activity can be encountered in these systems. They form an integral part of the natural environment of this land of lively creation.

From creatures to cultures, a spectacular integration of life!

Corn bird in flight from nest

This colourful zandoli lizard does a mating ritual on the rocks of Bloody Bay beach in Tobago

Dragon Fly perched with sunlit wings

A Blue Empress butterfly is held in the clutches of this scorpion on the hunt

Colourful sprays of lilies display great beauty rising from an unlikely location along the Betham just outside Port of Spain

An aerial view of the Caroni Swamp

The misty Caroni Swamp is the main habitat of the scarlet ibis, one of the national birds

Sea coconut on Manzanilla Beach

Man of war on Mayaro Beach

Blue Heron on Pigeon Point Beach

Land of the Double Chaconia

Without question, the colour of the nation must be red. It is dramatic and energetic, with an iridescent air. It is fiery and incandescent, radiating the very glow of life. The tone and tinge of this unmistakable red can be seen in the long, magnificent and regal sprays of the Chaconia, the national flower of Trinidad and Tobago. The botanical name of this majestic genus is *warszewiczia coccinea*, of the *rubianceae* family. Locally known as 'Wild Poinsettia' or 'Pride of Trinidad and Tobago', there are two distinct variants of this special flower found within these shores, the more generally known single Chaconia and the rare and mutant double Chaconia which is accepted as being unique to Trinidad and Tobago.

It is claimed by many that the flower was named the Chaconia in honor of Trinidad's last colonial Spanish Governor, Don Jose Maria Chacon, who is renowned for his tremendous work in the development of the island and its capital city, Port of Spain. There are those, however, who believe that the name originates from the French word *chaconne*, a folk dance in which the performers adorned their dresses with frills depicting the regal flower. With a seeming uncanny sense of nationalism, this ornamental evergreen is in annual bloom mid-year and by the 31st of August, the day that Trinidad and Tobago became independent from Great Britain in 1962.

A symbolic standard bearer, in colourful concert with the national flag, the Chaconia flower stands proudly signifying the bright history and the even brighter future prospects of the resplendent land of Trinidad and Tobago.

Ancient stalactite and stalagmite formations in Gasparee caves, Gasparee Island

The refreshing La Laja falls at Blanchisseuse

The beautiful spread of Matelot waterfalls

The splendid tropical brilliance of the hibiscus flower

The colourful blue-crowned motmot bird is one of many which delight avid bird-watchers

The natural wonder of the pitch lake in La Brea is known not just for its world famous asphalt, but also for its warm therapeutic sulphur springs and pools in which many often bathe

The Giant Leatherback Turtle

Trinidad and Tobago shares a remarkable oceanic phenomenon of having the unique coordinates of its global position indelibly etched into the navigational homing instincts of one of the world's largest marine creatures, the giant Leatherback Turtle. Of the Atlantic sub-population of this magnificent aquatic animal, there are four primary nesting locations in the entire Atlantic Ocean region – Suriname and French Guiana on the South American mainland, Gabon in Central Africa, and Trinidad and Tobago in the Caribbean. Nesting leatherbacks may be found in other locations, but in far fewer numbers than these preferred places. Leatherbacks are known to return to specific areas to breed every 2–3 years, finding their way back home after long periods in the depths of the ocean's vast environment.

Leatherback Sea Turtles, *Dermochelys coriacea*, have been on earth for millions of years, from the age of the dinosaur to present-day man. Their habitat spans the globe from the North Atlantic Ocean to the South Pacific. Leatherbacks are the largest of the turtle species. They can grow to lengths upward of 1.7m and weigh as much as 900kg. Estimates of their population in 1980 were over 115,000 adult females. However, present figures are now less than 25,000 worldwide. They are said to be close to extinction in the Pacific Ocean.

Trinidad and Tobago is therefore a privileged location in being able to host generations of Leatherback Turtles. The best site at which these phenomenal creatures may be seen is Grande Riviere. This small, rural village along Trinidad's northern coast is home to one of the world's most important leatherback sea turtle nesting beaches. Incredibly, though less than a mile long, this beach hosts more than 5,000 turtles per season and during peak periods will have more than 500 nests in a single night. For some observers, this beach is considered to be the most densely nested leatherback beach in the world. It is also one of the most visited turtle beaches in the world, with as many as 15,000 people coming each year, most of whom are locals. Equally

popular, and another prime nesting site in Trinidad is Matura Beach along the Northeastern coast. In Tobago, favoured nesting locations can be found at Back Bay, Black Rock, Grafton Beach and the aptly-named Turtle Beach.

Leatherbacks migrate hundreds of miles every year. It is only the females however which come back to land for short periods, as little as one and a half hours in many instances, to lay their eggs. Male leatherbacks never leave the water after entering it as hatchlings. Each female leatherback has the potential to nest up to ten times in one nesting season with each nest containing 65-130 eggs, and return every 3-4 years for as long as thirty years.

The Trinidad and Tobago Stock Exchange in Nicholas Towers on Independence Square, Port of Spain

Commerce & Industry

The enterprise of a nation is seen in the capacity of its industry and the product of its commerce.

Trinidad and Tobago continues to consolidate upon its geo-economic position in the Caribbean as a bustling hub of business activity with far reaching global impact. No mere sultry sand and sea atoll, this relatively tiny twin island nation carries a commercial weight of influence that includes being a primary supplier of the liquefied natural gas (LNG) imported by some of the largest foreign economies in the world, including the United States of America. Its success in commerce and industry lies not only in a focus on its natural hydro-carbon wealth, but on the development of vibrant and talented human assets.

The primary resource of any nation is its people. It is the quality of a country's citizens that most determines the quality of life in that nation. Fundamental to establishing the desired character of the population is the active human resource development paradigm. With a literacy rate exceeding 98% as determined by the United Nations Educational, Scientific and Cultural Organization (UNESCO), Trinidad and Tobago has an educated workforce which is highly ranked in the Caribbean. This particularly high level of proficiency can be attributed to its government making the provision of education readily accessible to all, from nursery to tertiary. With an appreciation of the strategic value of its people, the government of Trinidad and Tobago continues to articulate and enact key educational initiatives to facilitate the enhancement of its Human Resource capacity.

With a broad range of natural resources, chiefly featuring vast national reserves of oil and gas, the petrochemical endeavour is the foremost international revenue earning commodity package to the relatively thriving economy of Trinidad and Tobago. Whilst the hydrocarbon sector may be the industrial epicentre of business in the country, many other growing enterprises across the commercial spectrum are blossoming. Such activities include agriculture and agro-products; music and entertainment; arts and fashion; the film industry; food and beverages; fishing and seafood; leisure and merchant marine; and, printing and packaging.

A place of opportunity and prosperity, rewarding the output of the productive...!

Trinidad and Tobago enjoys a strategic geographical location that positively benefits its marketing and its marketability. As a nation of huge progressive ideals striving for its defined position on the modern international cutting edge, it is founded upon stable democratic governance and institutions. This nation offers an infrastructure that is constantly being consolidated. Evidence of this effect can be seen in world standard communication links, financial systems, and a multiplicity of new business conference facilities, especially at preeminent hotel lines. Trinidad and Tobago readily distinguishes itself as a financial centre and gateway to international business prospects. Indeed, many of the world's leading corporations are already engaged in huge commercial operations here. The local economy, guided by its principal national stakeholders, provides an operational arena that is particularly conducive to prime trade and investment opportunities to discerning investors locally, regionally and internationally. Whether east to west, north to south or on-shore

to off-shore, the evidence is empirical: business abounds in Trinidad and Tobago.

A place of opportunity and prosperity, rewarding the output of the prospecting and productive...!

View of the commercial centre of the city of Port of Spain

Grand Government Building, downtown Port of Spain

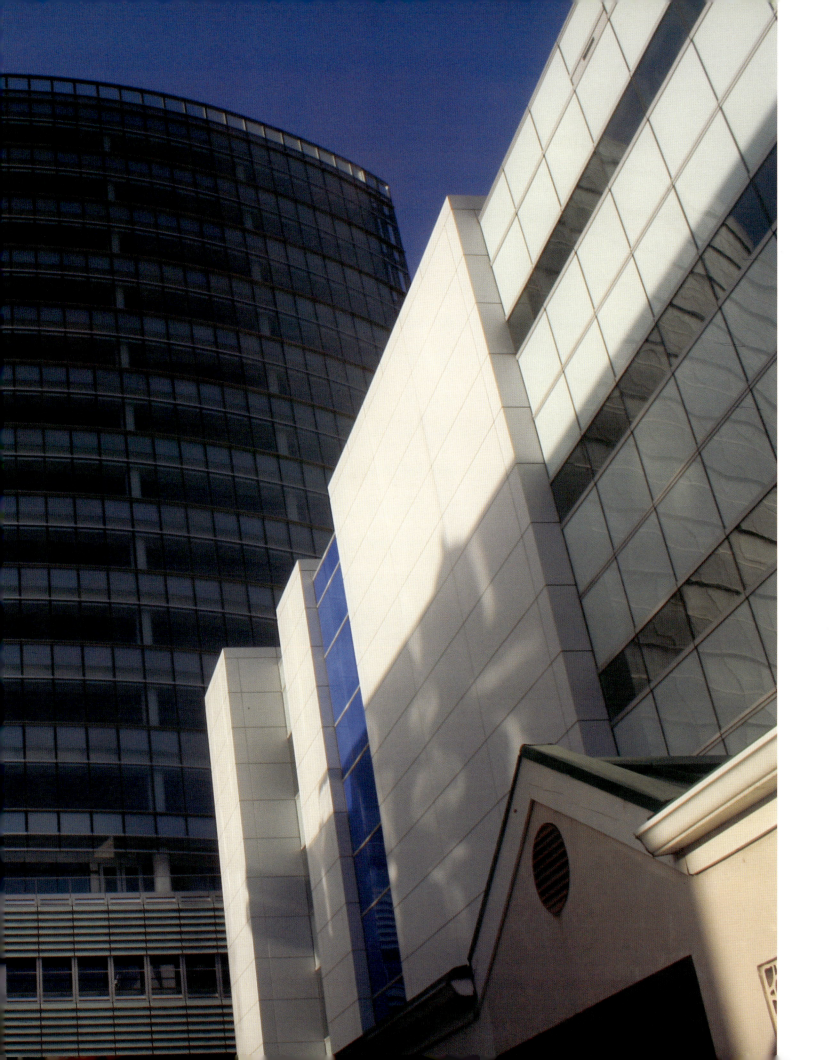

Pumping oil derricks in the oil fields of Forrest Reserve

Drilling for Oil since 1857

The verdant land of Trinidad and Tobago has long been found to be specially endowed with a wealth of natural resources and commercial opportunities. Over the centuries, prized national assets have attracted the interests of many entrepreneurial explorers whose invested business efforts have gained world impacting returns. From the 16th century onwards, the great plantation estates of sugarcane, cotton, indigo, coffee and cocoa turned out lucrative exports which became well known trading products and generated great consumer demand from distant international markets. None of these staple commodities however, as valuable as they were, would match the exploration yields from the rich, black, gooey substance called oil that would be found deep beneath the dark fertile soil of this relatively tiny landmass.

Many years before oil production became the bastion in global enterprise and economics which it is now known to be, pioneering engineers drilled prospecting wells into the heartland of Trinidad and Tobago. They were searching for laden subterranean repositories of this oil that was to become a primary product to fuel the industrial age. Out of these forward-looking penetrated holes made into the earth's depths gushed a petroleum industry that quickly rose into the mainstay of the nation's economy. Later years would affirm these seminal explorations which grew to such an extent making Trinidad and Tobago widely recognized as an energy producing country of significant world repute.

Unlike anywhere else, early oil explorers had reason to be drawn to Trinidad and Tobago because of the ancient tangible signs which suggested the presence of petroleum within its shores. One such indicator is the *'Pitch Lake'*, a magnificent world-wonder located just in-land from the coast of the northern side of the south-western peninsula. This geological phenomenon features a vast open reservoir of a heavy tar-like substance. Previously hidden in the heel of the Caribbean, it persuaded scientists and engineers that if this gummy hydrocarbon form was present in such great proportions, then its close relative, the silky flow of rich sweet crude, should also be found. With this driving perspective, history shows that in 1857, an American enterprise called the Merrimac Company drilled the first well at 280 feet into the earth hoping to strike oil near the Pitch Lake in La Brea. The Merrimac well is considered by many to be the first commercial drilling prospect in the world, though a well drilled in Pennsylvania, U.S.A., in 1859, by Colonel Edwin Drake is recognized as initiating the modern oil industry. Whilst that initial thrust of the Merrimac Company did not produce any oil, nine years later in 1866, and just a few short miles away from the La Brea site, at the Aripero Estate, an English civil engineer by the name of Walter Darwent, drilled the first productive well that flowed with good quality oil.

Walter Darwent's life is chronicled as that of a storied adventurer. He was born in Norfolk, England, in 1821. As a young man, he was trained in mechanical engineering working on the construction of bridges, railway tunnels and roads. He ventured to North America and fought in the American Civil War which began in 1861. He retired from the military as an army captain and was somehow drawn to Trinidad in 1865 to find oil. Perhaps inspired by certain operational demands he had seen in the war allied with his own engineering background, his interests were sparked toward the pursuits of finding oil reserves somewhere. He probably hoped to satisfy a military and an impending industrial need for a ready supply of fuel.

It is said that Darwent knew little about oil exploration but had a hunch that was keenly energized to find oil in Trinidad. Arriving in Trinidad and immediately setting about his mission, he had some early setbacks by drilling a couple dry holes. However, striking success at the Aripero site in 1866 propelled his hopes enormously with an expectation of finding sizeable deposits of oil in commercial quantities. Alas, in the midst of arrangements to expand his drilling operations, he contracted yellow fever and died in La Brea on September 28, 1868 at the age of forty-seven. Shortly after his death, in 1869 more oil was found near to the Darwent site in Aripero and in another nearby location called Guapo. The oil exploration achievement of Walter Darwent, without question, is one of the great pillars in the heritage of the development of the oil industry in Trinidad and Tobago. These initial tangible finds led to further large-scale discovery and development of oilfields at Forest Reserve, Point Fortin, Barrackpore and Tabaquite.

Commercial production of oil for export purposes in this Caribbean twin-island state did not begin in earnest until 1910, when the first cargo of crude left the Brighton port in La Brea. Trinidad and Tobago's first refinery was built in 1912, and by 1930 crude oil production reached 10 million barrels a year. With the

Miles of crude oil pipe-lines along the Forest Reserve – Point Fortin road

advancement of the petrochemical industry in more recent years, the discovery of Natural Gas has taken up the mantle as the key to the country's energy revenue future. Whilst there have been relatively few new discoveries of oil deposits lately, there have been substantial findings of gas, primarily from off-shore fields along Trinidad's east coast. As a result, industry growth has been fuelled by investments in liquefied natural gas (LNG), and other petrochemical derivatives like methanol and ammonia.

It is noteworthy that, as an energy producing nation, Trinidad and Tobago is recognized as one of the world's largest exporters of LNG, methanol and ammonia. Statistics show that in 2007, this small twin-island Caribbean nation accounted for some 60% of the United States' colossal demand for LNG. With an internationally recognized status as a significant oil and gas producing country, many of the world's major energy conglomerates and multinationals have operating bases in Trinidad and Tobago managing billion dollar investments.

To this present day, that first productive oil well in Trinidad and Tobago with its head valves now capped, remains on display as a national monument of industrial achievement at its location in the now rural residential village of Aripero. This well-head stands as vivid evidence of the early revolutionary oil exploration operations which forever mark Trinidad and Tobago's place in the annals of the global oil industry.

The sprawling oil refinery complex at Pointe-a-Pierre

Major highway arteries in and out of the city Port of Spain via the primary transportation hub of City Gate

International cargo handling at the port of Port of Spain

234

Agricultural farmlands in Caroni

The fruit of the land – Melons, pineapples, papayas, carambolas (star fruit) and mangoes

A large variety of home-grown produce on sale at the Chaguanas market

Casting the net from the pier at Pigeon Point, Tobago.

Pulling in the seine or fishing nets at Black Rock, Tobago

These Las Cuevas fishermen have their work cut out as they pull their boat up to the shore after a day at sea

This giant wahoo was caught during the International Big Game Fishing Tournament, an event held each year in March at the beautiful fishing village of Charlotteville in Tobago

Fish vendor at Charlotte Street Fish Market, Port of Spain

Fashion in Trinidad & Tobago

The strutting pizzazz of high fashion on the runways of Trinidad and Tobago! Caribbean couture clothing lines are featured by renowned local designers including Meiling, Peter Elias, Heather Jones and Anya Ayoung-Chee, the season nine winner of the internationally acclaimed television series Project Runway

Major cruise ships visit Trinidad and Tobago docking at the bustling port of Port of Spain

Sunrise over the marina at Chaguaramas

Sights & Scenes

The vistas of a nation's scenery highlight the spectacle of its identity.

From any vantage point within Trinidad and Tobago, there is always some prominent landscape feature that unmistakably stands out as a display to captivate the attention.

The scenery of this Caribbean twin island nation seems particularly suited to its population of spontaneous performers. The entire country appears as an enormous theatrical stage fitted with every imaginable stage prop and setting to facilitate every elaborate act and scene in the dramatic production that is called life in Trinidad and Tobago.

A typical 'down town' view of people about their routine business manifests the hustle and bustle of the daily life of a thriving nation. Whether in the city of Port of Spain in Trinidad, Scarborough in Tobago; or, any of the other towns across both islands, the colourful cast of the nation's populace creates a picturesque performance. The protagonists are varied. Distinctive Caribbean street scenes abound. They portray the general workforce of business people, vendors, shoppers, and the teeming tangle of traffic. Altogether, they weave intertwining plots in the midst of a frenetic framework of concurrent activities.

In contrast with the peopled scenes of the cities and the towns, the props and settings take on a dramatic change as you move 'out of town' to find yourself immersed in an ambience orchestrated by nature's peaceful air. At such locations, your encounter will include quiet coves and sultry beaches. Tobago's Pigeon Point, the Buccoo Reef and the Nylon Pool will match any seaside setting anywhere on earth for the wonderment of sheer beauty. See the caves at Gasparee Island with its ancient stalagmites and stalactites; or visit the Aripo cave and experience the sight and echo-locating clicks of the famed and near-blind *oilbirds*. In the southland of La Brea there is the visible marvel and starkness of the world renowned lake of pitch. Just outside Princes Town, you can witness the eerie bubbling mud volcanoes at the *Devil's Woodyard*. For the hiker there are numerous meandering trails in forested regions as in some lost world. In many of the rocky mountain locations there are torrents of gushing waterfalls creating crystalline streams, pools and rivers. All these and more remarkable and exhilarating sights reflect the more tranquil face on offer in the master presentation of this treasured paradise.

From dawn to dusk, the incredible landscape of Trinidad and Tobago has its daily rendezvous with the sun, sea and sky to create a perpetual panoramic performance that is truly glorious. It is said that the surroundings in which people exist affects the quality of their mood, which in turn affects their aesthetic judgment and behaviour. Perhaps, it is the natural habitat that most influences the typical *Trinbagonian*. For, being saturated by the allure of the local scenic splendour, one's senses cannot be but irresistibly soothed.

In the midst of it all, you can get away from it all...!

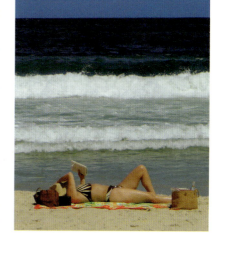

In the midst of it all, you can get away from it all...!

Sunset on the waves! Surfer walks the beach at Las Cuevas

Diego Martin, known fondly as "Diego" or the "Valley", is a popular suburb of Port of Spain

Enjoy the scenic seclusion of Pirate's Bay, Tobago

Statue of St. Peter, the patron saint of fisherman, looks over Seau D'eau beach, on the north coast

Down *d'islands* at Scotland Bay, a favourite weekend getaway

Caribbean Coconuts

A tropical coastal scene fringed with lines of coconut trees often conjures a certain sense of the romantic in some idyllic setting. These sultry palms in such classic locations are readily recognized by their slim, tall and elongated trunks. Their lofty crowns are leafy sprays which appear as tufts of thick large feathers extending outward in every direction from a central core. At their hearts where all their branches meet, their fruit suspend in bulbous clusters. Their movement seems never sudden, but always as a rolling sway fanned by seasonal trade-wind breezes.

The coconut, *cocos nucifera,* is a member of a large family of palms, *arecaceae*. It is said that throughout South America and the Caribbean there are some 550 species of palms which are indigenous to the region, a diversity that is second only to Asia. Of the Caribbean islands, the largest range of this plant form is found in Trinidad and Tobago. This occurrence may well be attributed to the fact that the twin-island state is the southern-most of the island chain, lying just seven miles east off the coast of the South American mainland. This geographical proximity is what perhaps accounts for the closer bio-system relation here than elsewhere in the Caribbean. In Trinidad and Tobago the vast variety of palms found across the island include: anare, cabbage palm, camwell, carat, gru-gru, manac, moriche, palmiste, roseau, silver thatch, timite, and wild gri-gri.

Unlike these numerous indigenous plants, the coconut palm is not a native of the Americas or the Caribbean; in fact it has its origins in Southeast Asia. In perhaps a very uncanny parallel, the coconut, which has become the most predominant palm found throughout the Caribbean, is somewhat like the people who now inhabit the region. Illustrated in Trinidad and Tobago, the population chiefly comprises people whose predecessors primarily came from eastern continents who over time came to replace the western aboriginals as the dominant races. Both the coconut and the migrant diasporas had to journey across vast oceans to arrive at shores across the Caribbean and the Americas. From trees afar off as the Ganges delta in India to the Polynesian Islands, many fallen coconuts found themselves afloat at sea being carried away by the dictates of master waves driven by great ocean currents. An occurrence not too dissimilar to the fate encountered by those forced passengers on past colonist's merchant ships. Both plant and people had to display their toughest resilience to survive. They were to preserve the kernel of their inherent identities in the face of harsh and treacherous conditions along their respective voyages to become new nationals in faraway lands.

Today, all across the Americas and in the adjacent 'Continent of Islands' (Mark Kurlansky, 1992) called the Caribbean, an abundance of coconut palms form a distinct coastline presence. They are very much at home in these western landscapes as their ancestors are in the east. Their inimitable picturesque poise is ubiquitous and unmistakable.

North coast view from hikers' trail

Fishing boat moored at King's Wharf, San Fernando

Las Cuevas Bay at sunset

The Ever Evolving Faces of the Races

The future of a nation can be seen in the faces of its children.

Perhaps the greatest visual spectacle to behold in Trinidad and Tobago is its people, and in particular, the children of the nation who represent a picture of a future filled with unlimited prospects. The many colourful faces of these sons and daughters of the soil indicate an assortment of races that is demonstrably Caribbean.

Trinidad and Tobago could certainly fit the universal definition of being called a multicultural society. However, given its particular fated combination of historical and social circumstances, there resides a certain tropical island synergy which has grafted and guided a distinctly vibrant fusion of cultures to create the unique *Trinbagonian* model. Its broad cosmopolitan distribution of ethnicities is a true reflection of a land once acclaimed as a "rainbow nation" by the world renowned peace activist, Archbishop Desmond Tutu of South Africa. Indeed the strands of colour which make up this symbol of unity are drawn from a people originating from distant lands around the world.

Where did the children of this nation originate? The faces of the nation's son and daughters clearly reflect a diversity of ethnicities which can be attributed to distant continents. How did they arrive? Multi-community societies are significantly influenced by migration. People have always been moving from one part of the world to another pursuing relocation to preferred places to live for one reason or other. The Caribbean has its own history concerning the migratory will of its people. It is quite distinct from other ethnically diverse countries elsewhere in the world. Illustrative of the Antillean Islands, Trinidad and Tobago has a population which comprises descendants of displaced Africans, Chinese, Europeans, East Indians and Middle Easterners, beside the indigenous Arawak and Carib descendants of the Amerindians of South America. For the Caribbean as a whole, the disparate races distributed across the islands have been classified collectively as *West Indians*.

...a picture of a single prosperous nation that is classically Trinbagonian

Born out of the will to survive, there is a national fortitude inherent in Caribbean people. It is a decided determination to ultimately prevail, regardless of the overwhelming odds of adversity being confronted. Whether actively or passively, this innate characteristic resides within the region's youth. It is a legacy from their forefathers who learned to overcome harsh experiences of forced migration in their time and have shown a remarkable capacity to adapt comparatively well in the face of this very sensitive balancing act. Despite intrinsic hurdles to spontaneous cultural collaboration, the national anthem of Trinidad and Tobago proudly pronounces and promotes the desired outcome with the line, *"Here every creed and race find an equal place."* Such an ideal would serve well in guiding all diverse societies.

Children can be said to be the present gateway between the cultural past and the cultural future. They carry the handed-down qualities of their elders, but in their lifetime, they build upon the existing foundation and all its inborn peculiarities to create an updated version of their identity that would affect their offspring. In many societies, the advent of every new generation is a significant contributor which promotes the acceptance of new ideals which build on the communal social experience. Younger persons, in the era in which they live, are often less rigid in adhering to the purist's perspective of traditional cultural values. They are more likely to embrace closer co-relations with their community peers. The innocence of youthful spontaneity is a great contributor to contemporary cultural unity.

The children of Trinidad and Tobago display more than just an eye-catching cultural portrait. They epitomize a resilience born of the continuous intertwining of the social threads which make up the fabric of the national tapestry. Therefore beyond the many pretty smiling faces, there is a picture of a single prosperous nation that is classically *Trinbagonian*.

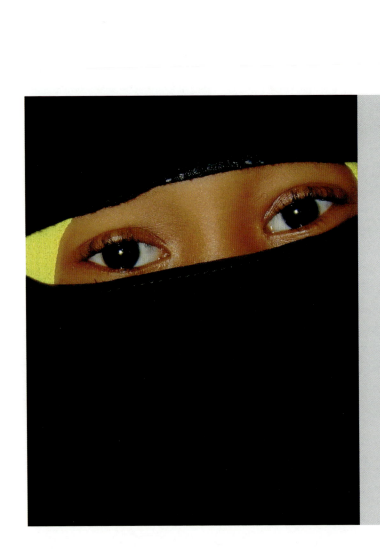

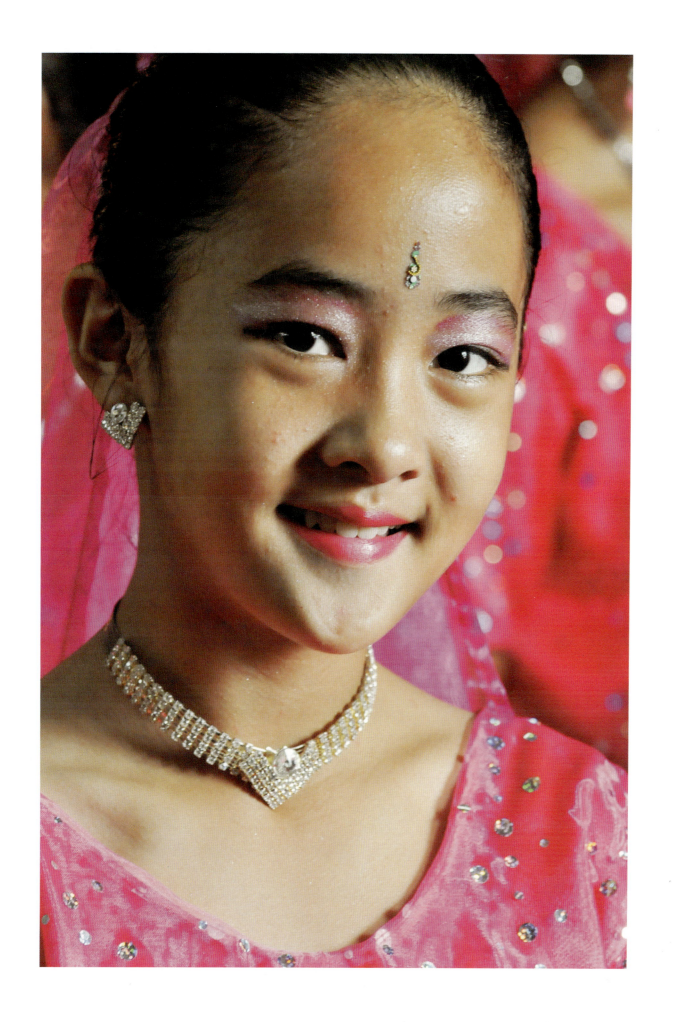

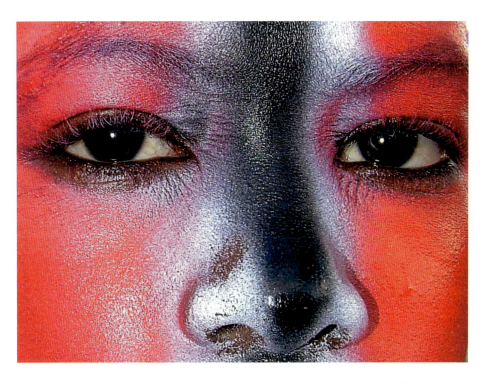

Sources & References

LITERATURE
- Charry, Eric. 1996. *A Guide to the Jembe;* University of North Carolina at Greensboro
- Comeau, Paul L. 2003. Comeau, Yasmin S.; and, Johnson, Winston ; *The Palm Book of Trinidad & Tobago including the Lesser Antilles;* International Palm Society
- Doumbia, Abdoul and Wirzbicki, Matthew. 2006. *Anke Djé Anke Bé - Djembe and Dounou Music from Mali, West Africa, Vol. 1;* 3idesign
- Foale, M. 2003. *The Coconut Odyssey: the bounteous possibilities of the tree of life;* Australian Centre for International Agricultural Research
- Gale, Thompson. 2005. *Gale Encyclopedia of Religion;* Jones, Lindsay, ed; ISBN ISBN 0-02-865980-5
- Hill, Errol. 1997. *The Trinidad Carnival,* New Beacon Books
- Kirton, Enid. 2008. *Caribbean Storyteller Classics,* Ealkirt Institute, San Fernando, Trinidad & Tobago
- Malone, Jacqui. 1996. *Steppin' on the Blues,* University of Illinois Press - page 10,11
- McDaniel, Lorna. 1999. *Garland Encyclopedia of World Music, Volume Two: South America, Mexico, Central America, and the Caribbean;* Routledge
- McGinley, Mark. 2010. Hogan, C.Michae; and, Cleveland, C.; eds.; *Petenes Mangroves - Encyclopedia of Earth. National Council for Science and the Environment;* Washington DC World Wildlife Fund
- Moodie-Kublalsingh, Sylvia. 1994. *The Cocoa Panyols of Trinidad: an oral record,* British Academic Press
- Munro, Martin. 2009. *The French Creoles of Trinidad and the Limits of the Francophone French Studies;* 63(2): 174-188
- Stewart, John. 2008. *Mission and Leadership Among the "Merikin" Baptists of Trinidad;* University of Illinois at Urbana
- Welsh, Kariamu. 2004. *African Dance;* Chelsea House Publishers pages 28 ISBN 0-7910-764155
- Winer, Lise. 2009. *Dictionary of the English/Creole of Trinidad & Tobago,* McGill-Queen's University Press; Bilingual edition

INTERNET
- Carnival Riots, Original Correspondence of the British Colonial Office in London (C.O. 884/4, Hamilton Report into the Carnival Riots, p.18), Trinidad Sentinel 6 August, 1857: http://www.xklsv.org/viewwiki.php?title=Hosay. Retrieved May 12, 2011
- Coconut - Concise Oxford Dictionary (tenth ed.). Oxford: Clarendon Press. ISBN 0-19-860287-1, J. Pearsall, ed., 1999; http://www.sources.com/SSR/Docs/SSRW-Coconut.htm. Retrieved August 13, 2011
- Dictionary of Trinidad - Chateau Guillaumme - http://cguillaumme.caribsurf.net/dictionary.html. Retrieved March 23, 2011
- Gatka, Dhankara; A Traditional Dance on Punjab, http://www.sadapunjab.com/punjabi/dhankara-gatka-a-traditional-dance-on-punjab.html. Retrieved June 30, 2011
- Government of Trinidad and Tobago Human Resource Services Company Limited, Maraval, Trinidad and Tobago; http://ghrs.gov.tt/. Retrieved January 21, 2011
- Hahn, William J.; Arecanae - The palms, tolweb.org, http://tolweb.org/Arecanae/21337. Retrieved August 13, 2011
- Mama Dis is Mas: A Historical Overview of the Trinidad Carnival, 1783 – 1900. http://carnivalculture.blogspot.com/2007/04/t-carnival-history.html. Retrieved May 17, 2011
- Ministry of Tourism, Port-of-Spain, Trinidad and Tobago, http://www.tourism.gov.tt/. Retrieved September 9, 2011
- Multicultural Society - http://www.triastelematica.org/. Retrieved January 21, 2011
- Oilbirds - Map of Life, Department of Earth Sciences, University of Cambridge, Downing St, Cambridge, Cambridgeshire, CB2 3EQ, United Kingdom; http://www.plosone.org/article/info:doi%2F10.1371%2Fjournal.pone.0008264. Retrieved June 14, 2011
- Republic of Trinidad and Tobago, Biodiversity Clearing House - http://www.trinbagobiodiversity.gov.tt/trees/index.htm. Retrieved August 13, 2011
- Sale, Alessandro and Luschi, Paolo; Navigational challenges in the oceanic migrations of leatherback sea turtles, http://rspb.royalsocietypublishing.org/content/276/1674/3737.short. Retrieved January 12, 2012
- Slavery Abolition Act 1833; Section XII. 1833-08-28. http://www.pdavis.nl/Legis_07.htm. Retrieved March 23, 2011
- The Leatherback Trust, Inc., 161 Merion Avenue, Haddonfield, New Jersey 08033, USA; http://www.leatherback.org/. Retrieved January 12, 2012
- Tobago House of Assembly, Act No. 37 of 1980; http://www.tha.gov.tt/. Retrieved September 9, 2011
- Warszewiczia coccinea, "Double Chaconia"; http://www.quentrall.com/Charity/Garden_Club/GG_Documents/Articles/Johnny%20Lee/Double%20Chaconia/GC_Double%20Chaconia.htm. Retrieved July 23, 2012

INTERVIEWS
- Balkaransingh, Satnarine. The Nrityanjali Theatre Inc. of Trinidad and Tobago. Interviewed July 7, 2012
- Kirton, Joyce. Les Enfants Dance Company of Trinidad and Tobago. Interviewed January 27, 2011
- Mahatoo, Indira. The Indira Mahatoo Dance Company of Trinidad and Tobago. Interviewed July 9, 2012